D1487919

eBay Inventory the Smart Way

Other Books by Joseph T. Sinclair
eBay the Smart Way, Fourth Edition
eBay Business the Smart Way, Second Edition
eBay Motors the Smart Way
eBay Global the Smart Way
Building Your eBay Traffic the Smart Way
eBay Photography the Smart Way

eBay Inventory
the Smart Way

How to Find Great Sources and Manage Your Merchandise to
Maximize Profits on the World's #1 Auction Site

Joseph T. Sinclair
and
Jeremy Hanks

ᴀMACOM

American Management Association
New York • Atlanta • Brussels • Chicago • Mexico City • San Francisco
Shanghai • Tokyo • Toronto • Washington, D.C.

Codman Sq. Branch Library
690 Washington Street
Dorchester, MA 02124-3511

SEP - - 2006

Special discounts on bulk quantities of AMACOM books are available to corporations, professional associations, and other organizations. For details, contact Special Sales Department, AMACOM, a division of American Management Association, 1601 Broadway, New York, NY 10019.
Tel.: 212-903-8316. Fax: 212-903-8083.
Web site: www.amacombooks.org

This publication is designed to provide accurate and authoritative information in regard to the subject matter covered. It is sold with the understanding that the publisher is not engaged in rendering legal, accounting, or other professional service. If legal advice or other expert assistance is required, the services of a competent professional person should be sought.

Library of Congress Cataloging-in-Publication Data

Sinclair, Joseph T.
    EBay inventory the smart way : how to find great sources and manage your merchandise to maximize profits on the world's #1 auction site / Joseph T. Sinclair and Jeremy Hanks.
      p. cm.
    Includes index.
    ISBN 0-8144-7359-8
    1. eBay (Firm) 2. Internet auctions. 3. Internet marketing. I. Hanks, Jeremy. II. Title.
    HF5478.S4739 2006
    658.8'7--dc22   2005033864

© 2006 Joseph T. Sinclair.
All rights reserved.
Printed in the United States of America.

This publication may not be reproduced, stored in a retrieval system, or transmitted in whole or in part, in any form or by any means, electronic, mechanical, photocopying, recording, or otherwise, without the prior written permission of AMACOM, a division of American Management Association, 1601 Broadway, New York, NY 10019.

Printing number
10 9 8 7 6 5 4 3 2 1

To all the entrepreneurial eBay retailers who take risks, work hard, persist, and bring success to their suppliers, eBay, themselves, and their families. You are pioneers in exciting new enterprises, and the world salutes you.

Joseph T. Sinclair

Jeremy Hanks

Contents

Acknowledgments

Bob Charlton, a search engine optimization guru, was helpful with certain issues in the chapter on research. And a warm thanks to him.

Thanks also to Anne Carson, poet, novelist, and translator of Classical Greek who informed me that the ancient Greeks invented "How To" books. The Greeks normally read on scrolls of papyrus. But in addition, they used folded pieces of papyrus that they carried around with them: that is, practical books with practical information. They called these books *encheiridion* (literally "hand books"). Thus we learn that as author and reader we are carrying on a practice that is thousands of years old.

As always, thanks to Carole, my agent, who does a great job, and to AMACOM.

A special thanks goes to my co-author Jeremy Hanks and his colleagues at Doba who were very supportive in making this book relevant and useful to eBay sellers.

And finally, to Lani and our children, Brook and Tommy, thank you for sharing the sacrifice it takes to complete a book project. It's not an 8-5 job.

Joseph T. Sinclair

Thanks to Brandon Williams and David Gray, two amazing entrepreneurs and leaders, and the best business partners that I could have.

Thanks also to Clark Winegar for your hard work on the book. Without your help and dedication, Doba would not be where it is.

And thanks to Stuart Lisonbee, Ryan Roberts, and Jeff Knight for your suggestions and contributions to the book.

Thanks to the entire Doba team. Your continued dedication and hard work humble me on a daily basis.

And finally, to my wife Amy and our daughter Kaitlin, thank you so much for your amazing support of my entrepreneurial endeavors. You let me chase my dreams, an for that I am truly grateful.

Jeremy Hanks

I

Introduction

1

Identifying, Choosing, and Finding Something to Sell

Determining what you are going to sell is one of the first steps to take in starting your eBay business. Equally important is figuring out where and how to find the items that you want to sell. For those who already have an eBay retail business, this chapter will help you approach the task of finding new inventory in a systematic way. Indeed, this chapter is an overview that abstracts the ideas you need to select your inventory intelligently. Then, starting with Chapter 9, the book collects and elaborates on individual ideas for acquiring inventory. But there is much to consider before you get that far.

Sources of Product Ideas

Later in this book is a series of chapters that lists various inventory sources. However, you need to decide before proceeding what types of products you desire to sell. The following sections will give you a good start on getting ideas suitable for your own situation.

Personal Experience

Most people who start a retail business on eBay, or online, start with products they know and understand from their own personal experience. That personal experience may be a job, a hobby, or another activity that entails buying and selling products. For instance, if you had a job working for a restaurant supply company selling kitchen supplies, it would be a natural for you to sell similar kinds of equipment on eBay. And there is a consumer demand for such professional equipment.

If your hobby is buying and selling antique dolls, then buying and selling antique dolls and other related collectibles on eBay would be a natural for you.

And finally, if one of your activities is horseback riding, buying and selling tack on eBay would be a natural for you.

What's the common denominator of all these activities? By being involved in these activities, you know the following:

- The various products associated with the activity
- The quality of various brands
- The dollar value of new and used items
- How the products are used
- How the products are bought and sold, and what guarantees and warranties are given in the transactions
- How the products are financed
- The size of market for the products (i.e., the number of potential customers)

It's this kind of knowledge and more that will enable you to be successful as an eBay retailer. It is also this background knowledge that will give you the confidence to get off to a good start and do a good job with your new eBay retail business.

That is not to say that you cannot start an eBay retail business without this kind of personal experience, but most people find that a good starting point for creating a retail business is based upon their own experience and knowledge with certain types of products.

Keep a Clear Head

Don't fall in love with a product. It's OK to be enthusiastic about the products you carry, but you have to be objective too. A good product for your inventory is one that you can sell for a good profit margin on eBay or elsewhere online. Assess the demand for each product you sell—before you start selling it, if possible. Read Chapter 27 for research information.

Buying

When most people begin to get involved in a new activity, they start buying the products needed to sustain such an activity. Although many people are careless buyers who tolerate wasting money and even tolerate low quality products, most of us do the best we can to research the markets and get the highest quality products for the lowest possible prices. This process of evaluating quality and pricing products at the beginning of a new activity sometimes takes a lot of research. It is exactly this kind of research that will make you an expert on such products. Therefore, being a buyer is a good start on opening the door to establishing your eBay retail business.

In fact, many people, in going through such a buying exercise, discover that there are niches in the market that have not yet been filled by anybody. They find products for which they believe there's a demand that has not yet been satisfied on eBay. Or perhaps certain products are not yet available on eBay with the variety that should be available. Thus, if you do your buying carefully and energetically, you will often discover niches that you otherwise would never know existed.

We (the authors) always buy as much as we can on eBay not only to get a wide selection and good prices, but also to keep in touch with the vast eBay market. In doing so, we run across ideas for potential niche markets all the time that present great opportunities for others who will discover them just as we have discovered them.

Supplementing Existing Inventory

Those of you who already have an eBay business are invariably interested in supplementing your existing inventory or perhaps even starting new lines of products. The most logical approach for you to take is to find similar products that have similar consumer markets. That will enable you to sell the new products to your existing customers.

Hence, if you are selling touring bicycles on eBay, you might want to consider selling such things as tents and lightweight cooking utensils for people who will take their bikes on long cross-country tours. Tents and lightweight cooking utensils are not necessarily bicycle accessories, but many people who take bicycling seriously are outdoor types who might be likely to go on a cross-country bicycle tour and camp out each night.

Accessories

The obvious related products for you to seriously consider selling are accessories to the products you are already selling. So using the bicycle example from above, you can see that the following accessories might be good additions to your product line:

- Clothing designed for bicyclists
- Bicycle racks for carrying things on bicycles
- Bicycle helmets
- Bicycle lights
- Tire repair kits
- Bicycle racks for cars

And the list is endless. Many products have a long list of accessories, and you can expand your inventory to carry them profitably because you already have a group of customers in your database who are likely to buy such accessories. Then, too, the future customers of your existing products are also likely to buy such accessories.

Customer Service

Some accessories are inexpensive and perhaps not worth your trouble to handle. However, providing such accessories to your customers is a type of customer service, which may be an overriding consideration in determining whether such accessories are worth selling. In addition, if you can sell such accessories as a package with your existing products so that you don't have to sell them separately, your handling cost is less and the dollar amount to which you can sell each customer is higher.

Parts

Parts are like accessories. You can sell them to your existing customers. After all, your customers are the ones who may need parts for routine maintenance and repairs. Depending on the product and the market, you may want to sell either new parts or used parts or even both. In any case, parts seem a logical and reasonable choice for acquiring and selling additional inventory.

The parts business is pretty good on eBay Motors (*http:// www.motors.ebay.com*) and for other sections of eBay as well. There's a good chance it will work for your retail business if your products are repairable.

Sets

Parts are for when something breaks. But many products have consumables, accessories or parts that get consumed or lost and have to be replaced routinely. For example, you buy a hand-powered labeling machine at an eBay Store. It comes with three rolls of labeling tape. You use all the tape and need some more. You order a three-roll pack for $2.35 from the eBay store. The shipping and handling is $3. You've just paid over double. If, however, the eBay retailer offers you a set of six three-roll packs for $11 and the shipping and handling is $3, you will probably be a happy camper.

So offer consumables in sets that make sense. Even if consumables can't be sold gracefully on eBay one at a time, they might be a profitable addition to your inventory if you sell them in sets.

Small Bulk

The ultimate logical extension of selling in sets is selling in bulk. If you go to the supermarket, you can buy rolls of paper towels one at a time as you need them. You can even buy a set of three. But if you want to buy them in bulk, you will probably go to Costco and buy a carton of 12. If you're an eBay retailer, why not sell in bulk?

We're not talking big bulk here like a big business might buy. We're talking small bulk like a person might buy if given the opportunity. For instance, Joe likes to keep his life simple by wearing the same kind of socks every day. He has 30 pairs of synthetic white athletic socks all exactly the same. (Dress is casual in California.) About once a year, he buys a new set of 30. In other words, he buys in bulk. However, he would prefer gray socks. He has been looking on eBay for two years for synthetic gray athletic socks to buy in bulk and has not been able to find an offering for more than a set of three. He continues to look.

This is not a strategy that will work for all products, but if it applies to the products you sell, it's worth a try.

Full-Service Retailing

Speaking of accessories and parts, what about a full-service approach to retailing? A full-service retailer is one that sells certain primary products and *all* the accessories, parts, and services to support such products. We have seen little of this approach on eBay. It seems that few eBay retailers sell more than a modest portion of all the products they could sell to support their primary products.

There are certainly many offline retailers that run full-service stores profitably. Yet online would seem to be a more appropriate market for such an approach. Perhaps most eBay retailers don't have the capital to take the full-service approach, or perhaps they are satisfied to cherry-pick products based on profitability. Whatever the reason, there seem to be plenty of opportunites for full-service retailing in many niches.

Once you decide to become a full-service retailer, of course, coming up with inventory ideas isn't difficult. You simply stock all the accessories and parts necessary for consumers' full use of your primary products.

Intangibles

Not many eBay retailers consider the sale of intangibles. But intangibles such as warranties and service contracts are not only products; they are often both easy to sell and profitable. There are a number of companies that will enable you to sell warranties to your customers to cover their purchases, and at the same time provide you with a significant additional profit. Usually the warranties are provided by third-party vendors; that is, the company providing the warranty is not the wholesaler or manufacturer that provides the product. Rather, it is another company that is just in the business of providing the warranty or service contract. Thus, unless you seek out such companies, you probably will not even realize that they exist.

Keep in mind, that warranties and service contracts provided by third-party vendors may not actually provide warranties and services directly to the customers in the case of a claim. They may just pay the manufacturer to provide a replacement product or pay a repair facility to do the repairs and maintenance. That should be of no concern to you. The idea here is to provide extra protection for your customers and collect a fee for doing so from a third-party provider.

Added Value

Some retailers are what is called a *value-added reseller* (VAR). In many industries this is known as *value-add*. That is, the retailer provides some kind of value in addition to just providing the product itself. Sometimes this value is installing the product, training the buyer to use the product, or providing some other sort of service to enable the buyer to use the product. Of course, not all products need this sort of added value. But many products do. Because you should be an expert in the products you sell, you are the logical person to provide the added value. And the added value is something for which you may be able to charge and make additional profit. Indeed, the added value is in and of itself a viable product.

Common Added Value

For many products, the added value is free. This practice is prevalent in situations where the sales of the products are strictly limited to VARs (i.e., dealers) that provide the added value but sell the products at full retail prices. The products are not available anywhere at discount prices. For example, this is a common practice in the business software industry.

Sometimes the added value is a matter of customer service. Usually the added value, which you provide free, just covers getting the customer started with a product and nothing more. But just because somebody bought a product from you doesn't mean that you're obligated to provide consulting and maintenance services for the life of the product. So don't confuse the idea of value-added with customer service. Customer service is something that you provide *initially* at no cost to get the customer off to a good start.

For instance, let's say that you sell an electrical generator powered by a one-horsepower gasoline engine made in China. You sell quite a few of these on eBay because they are less expensive than most competing products. As a matter of customer service, you may write your own owner's manual for using this product, since the English version provided by the Chinese manufacturer is incomplete and poorly written.

Because you are an expert in this product, or should be, writing such a manual should be easy and quick for you to do. (You will, of course, have someone edit it.) This is good customer service. However, it's not really a value-added type of offering. It's not something you can easily charge a fee for, because your customers will likely feel it's something that should accompany the product without any additional payment.

On the other hand, you can provide maintenance service for this generator as part of a value-added package. For instance, you might offer a service which obligates you to provide maintenance supplies and advice for the next three years. Thus, you would send the buyer routine maintenance supplies as requested. You would also provide maintenance advice by telephone. You might include this in the price of the product—particularly if there are no discount sales of the product in the market—or you might sell a maintenance contract up front (and get your money up front too).

Part of a maintenance service could be that, at the end of the second and third year, the customer can remove the carburetor from the gasoline engine and send it into you for cleaning and tuning. For many products, the entire product can be sent in inexpensively for cleaning, adjusting, tuning, and other sorts of maintenance procedures. Obviously, for large and heavy products, this won't work well outside your locale. Yet for smaller products, there is an opportunity to provide maintenance services for the product and make extra money.

Naturally, to provide such services you have to get set up to actually perform the maintenance. So you will have to determine ahead of time exactly how you are going to do that and make it profitable.

A Value-Added Thing

Does the added value have to be a service? No. The added value can simply be another product—usually something more than an accessory—that you add to the primary product and deliver simultaneously.

Finding Inventory in the Abstract

If you are just fishing for potential products to sell on eBay and do not want to start your retail business based on your own experience and expertise, you are at a substantial disadvantage. Whatever products you think might work for you will require your considerable research to know whether they can, in fact, be sold profitably in a way that's acceptable to you. In other words, you have to become an expert in the product and the market for the product. You need to know how it's used, just as if you had been in business selling the product or had used it in one of your activities. There are no shortcuts here. If you start selling a product without knowing these things, you will be operating in the dark. Operating in the dark is usually not conducive to earning profits and may be a recipe for incurring surprising financial losses.

Again, the best way to research products is to buy them. If you're going to be a good eBay retailer, you need to buy the products, and in doing so, you will learn a lot about the products and the market.

If you want to go through the exercise of buying products without actually spending money on them, eBay provides you with a marketplace where you can do that easily. For instance, you can watch the bidding on a product without bidding on it yourself. You can even contact the seller for extra information indicating that you might bid if the information serves your purposes. Or you can otherwise gather information on the products without actually bidding on them or buying them. Naturally, you will want to follow through to the end of the auctions to see what the winning bids are.

In addition, you can go into the eBay archives which cover past auctions to determine what the products or similar products sold for on eBay. Using the Completed Listings filter will show you all the auctions that have been closed.

Of course, your research should not be limited to eBay. There's plenty of information elsewhere on most products including on other ecommerce websites, magazines, advertising, and other informational sources. In addition, there may be some technology that is essential for using the product that you must also master before you can expect to be a successful eBay retailer.

For instance, do you really want to sell tennis supplies without being a tennis player? Our advice to you is that if you don't play tennis and you want to sell tennis supplies on eBay to serious tennis players, get a racket and some balls and go out and play a little tennis.

Although it's tough to pick a new (to you) product to sell, this has certainly been done by a lot of people both on eBay and off. Our message in this section is simply that if you take this approach to starting an eBay retail business, do your homework. Chapter 27 can help you.

Other Considerations

Sometimes the perfect products are eliminated or altered by specific considerations. You need to cover all the bases.

Product Cycle

The following illustrates a generic sales cycle for a product. With hundreds of thousands of different products on eBay manufactured by tens of thousands of different manufacturers, there is no one-size-fits-all product cycle. Nonetheless, the following outline will give you some ideas to help you understand the product cycles of the items you hope to carry.

Your job is to compare the risks and rewards of selling a product wherever it is in its cycle and to anticipate future opportunities to sell the product profitably as its cycle progresses.

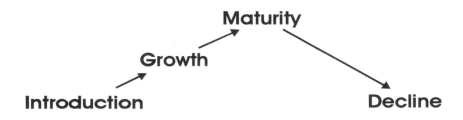

Figure 1.1 Product cycle illustrated.

Product Introduction

The product begins its retail life.

Price The price starts low or high depending on the manufacturer's strategy. Usually the introduction price is high, as the manufacturer attempts to recoup its development cost as quickly as possible. Sometimes for new products expected to have a mass market, a manufacturer sells first at a low price in order to gain market penetration quickly. Soon thereafter, it raises the price to a normal high introductory level.

Availability Initially, availability is limited. Not all wholesalers and retailers carry the product until the sales prove the success of the product. The manufacturer may not achieve full production capacity during this period.

Promotion Initial advertising and promotion is limited and aims at early adopters. Sometimes, however, a manufacturer conducts an expensive initial campaign to gain immediate market penetration.

Risk The product may bomb, leaving retailers with inventory they can't sell at a profitable price.

Opportunity The opportunity for retailers is to get in on the ground floor of selling a profitable new product; that is, get a jump on the retail competition.

Product Growth

The sales of a successful product grow.

Price If the price was initally high, it slowly declines. If the price was initially low, it increases to a normally high introductory price and then starts to slowly decline as sales grow. If growth is fast, the price may stabilize at a high level.

Availability As consumers accept the product, production volume increases, and more wholesalers and retailers (more channels) begin to carry the product.

Promotion The advertising and promotion now increases and aims at the entire consumer market for the product.

Opportunity This is an opportunity to start selling a new product that has gone a long way toward proving its popularity.

Risk A lot of other retailers will jump in to carry the product at this point. The sales of the product may abruptly quit growing and not reach its anticipated potential. Or the market could become flooded with competing products of higher quality, lower price, or both.

Product Maturity

The product gains a sales plateau.

Price The price stabilizes. Discount pricing by discount outlets starts to increase.

Availability The product achieves its widest distribution and in some cases may even include some non-traditional (for that type of product) retailers.

Promotion The advertising and promotional effort is healthy and uses a wide variety of techniques.

Opportunity This is now a proven product, easy to sell to consumers.

Risk The competition usually rises to the occasion. Other manufacturers start making competing products, and wholesalers and retailers compete vigorously. High-volume discounters become interested in thc product and start carrying it.

Product Decline

The sales of the product decline due to obsolescence or competition from higher-quality or lower-priced products.

Price The price begins to decline because supply is greater than demand.

Availability Some wholesalers and retailers no longer carry the product. The manufacturer cuts back or ceases production.

Promotion Advertising and promotional campaigns decline as sales no longer support them.

Opportunity Closeouts provide an opportunity to buy dirt cheap yet sell profitably at a deep discount from the normal retail price. The ranks of competing retailers thin out.

Risk Bargain pricing abounds. If you have purchased your inventory at a normal wholesale price, closeouts sold to your competitors may then decimate your sales. Demand may decline much faster than supply, swamping the market with unsalable merchandise.

Your Understanding

Your understanding of where your products are in their market cycles will enable you to better develop profitable retail sales strategies. It will also help you to spot opportunities for temporary or even ongoing profitable sales.

How do you research a specific product's product cycle? The quickest way is to become familiar with the industry, learn the history of the industry, learn the history of predecessor or similar products, become familiar with all the products in the industry, talk with others in the industry (manufacturers and wholesalers), and talk with colleagues (other retailers). That will give you a good idea. You can also search for sales data.

Drop Shipping Tip

Just for the record, Jeremy says that most successful drop shipping products are in the product *growth* and product *maturity* phases.

Availability

Products that you want to sell must be available to you. There may be governmental restrictions on some products that you will not be able to sell because you do not have the requisite license or you are unqualified to sell. For instance, you will probably not be able to sell nuclear devices on eBay without getting a license from the Atomic Energy

Commission (the AEC). That is an obvious example, but as we all know, the federal government, state governments, and local governments regulate many products and services and grant many licenses. You will want to make sure that your products are ones that can be sold within the scope of a license that you will be able to acquire if a license is required by a government entity to sell such products.

In addition, there will be manufacturers and wholesalers that will not sell to you. There are many reasons for this. One reason is that you may be too small. They may like to sell to large and established retailers. A second reason is that they might have dealer exclusives. In other words, they only sell to retailers that cover a certain limited territory. If they already have a retailer in your locale, they won't sell to you. Another reason is that some manufacturers and wholesalers are fussy about the type of retailers they do business with. For example, if they have high-class products and they perceive your retail operation as being low-class, they might refuse to sell to you. The reasons go on and on.

Thus, once you pick a product that you think will be the basis of a sound eBay retail business, you will want to immediately research whether you can acquire that product from a manufacturer or wholesaler for your retail sales. In addition, you will need to determine whether you will need some special permission or license from a government entity to sell such products. The fact is, you may find that there are some products that just simply are not available to you.

Offline Requirement

Some manufacturers and wholesalers will sell to you only if you have an offline (physical) retail location. Thus, you will have to operate a retail store in your locale in order to get the merchandise you need to sell the products on eBay. This is a common requirement. Joe knows one successful retailer who sells big time on eBay and makes a ton of money but is required to run a store in his town just to get inventory. His store brings in only 10 percent of his gross revenue.

Cost-Effectiveness

When you're in business, cost-effectiveness is always a consideration for everything you do, including choosing products to sell. Cost-effectiveness is covered in the next chapter, so we will not dwell on it here. But keep in mind that even for such a mundane task as choosing the types of products you want to sell, cost-effectiveness is a consideration.

Product Profit Model

Creating a product profit model is a means of evaluating a product to determine whether it's one that you should sell based on your own personal situation. You create this model in the abstract and then apply it to products that you have decided you might want to sell. It also helps you search for appropriate products. Chapter 3 covers it, and you will want to be aware of it when you're in the process of choosing products to sell for your eBay retail business.

Beware the Flood

You don't want to buy from a wholesaler that currently sells the same products to 40 other eBay retailers. That spells potential financial disaster. Rather, find a situation where there appears to be little interest from other eBay retailers and the eBay market is not saturated with retail sales of the products you intend to sell.

Be Flexible

The ideal niche to find will be one in which the products sell well on eBay (at a profit) and you have an exclusive on obtaining the inventory. That's a long shot. Consequently, your experience is more likely to be finding niches that prove profitable for a while and then get too crowded or otherwise decline. Then it's on to something else.

Thus, as you look ahead to a career as an eBay businessperson, it pays to be nimble. If you can find something to sell temporarily that has a high likelihood of success (profit), don't pass up the opportunity. In the future, a good percentage of the opportunities for selling on eBay may be temporary ones. Be prepared to move quickly and try new ideas.

On the Other Hand

Selling value-added products may generate more stable sales. Why? Because presumably not everyone can supply the added value. If you can, that may give you the edge you need to beat your competition.

Finding Inventory Opportunities

This chapter provides you with ideas about finding products that you can sell profitably on eBay. It reflects an approach that many prospective eBay entrepreneurs take to starting an eBay retail business. But it's not the whole story. Read Chapter 27 for more information about the research approach to determining what products you should sell on eBay.

Product Sourcing

When you look for products (inventory) to sell, it's called *product sourcing* or just *sourcing*. That's a term we don't use in this book much, but when you run across it here and elsewhere, you'll know what it means. Product sourcing is what we cover in Chapters 9 through 27.

About the Authors

Joseph T. Sinclair

Joe has worked in small businesses for 30 years, including retail businesses. He has written about Internet business and technology for ten years. He wrote his first book about eBay in 1999. This is his seventh eBay title (see the others in the Epilogue). Joe attends the eBay annual conferences, keeps current on eBay business and technology, and interviews many successful eBay retailers. He lives in the San Francisco Bay Area.

Jeremy Hanks

Jeremy is co-founder and CEO of Doba (formerly Wholesale Marketer), the premier drop shipping service for eBay retailers. Doba is an eBay Certified Service Provider, an eBay Certified Developer, and a member of the PayPal Merchant Advisory Council.

Jeremy's prior experience includes the development of numerous businesses in supply, wholesale distribution, and retail sales. He founded GearTrade.com, an online marketplace for used and distressed inventory.

Jeremy is an eBay PowerSeller, an eBay Educational Specialist trained by eBay, and an eBay Certified Consultant. He lives in Utah near Salt Lake City.

What This Book Covers

This book *really is* about finding inventory to sell in your eBay retail business. It isn't a book about starting an eBay retail business. You can find plenty of information on that topic in *eBay Business the Smart Way,* Second Edition (a book written for beginning eBay retailers) and also other books in the *eBay the Smart Way* series. Read more about these books in the Epilogue.

There are over 25 million items for sale on eBay today. That represents tens of thousands of product categories and millions of individual items. Each product has its own economic and marketing characteristics that differ as widely as does human consumption.

There is no way on Earth that a book like this can cover even a small fraction of products in accurate individual detail, and we make no attempt to do so. This is a book of generalities and ideas, as it must be. Regardless of what you sell, you will find plenty of profitable practices and ideas here relevant to your inventory. But be forewarned also, not every idea and practice here will necessarily be relevant to your particular retail inventory.

There is no silver bullet, no one-size-fits-all action plan for finding profitable inventory to sell. Like any other business, an eBay business is hard work. And part of the hard work is doing your homework regarding finding inventory that fits your retail aspirations. This is *sprechgesang* that you will hear again later.

More Than eBay

What a book covers is a matter of the authors' philosophy. It has been the philosophy of the *Smart Way* books to cover only important marketplaces. For instance, the first book in the eBay series, *eBay the Smart Way,* covered only eBay auctions. It did not cover Amazon or Yahoo auctions because eBay had over a 90 percent market share of the online auction business.

In subsequent years, Google, as the leading search engine with a market share of over 50 percent, emerged as a powerful de facto marketplace. It also created Froogle, a relatively new marketplace, which continues to expand and even features many eBay items. In the meanwhile, Craig's List, which started about the same time as eBay, now successfully runs local marketplaces in over 100 cities in the United States and abroad.

Because it is so easy and inexpensive for eBay retailers to participate in these additional marketplaces (after some setup work), it doesn't make sense to ignore them. Indeed, *Building Your eBay Traffic the Smart Way* covers the means of marketing in several substantial marketplaces (e.g., Froogle) simultaneously. Fortunately, finding inventory for eBay is identical to finding inventory for Froogle and other marketplaces.

You can take all your items for sale on eBay and also sell them on Froogle with little additional cost or work after some setup effort. Of course, you will want to do that. Google-Froogle (and potentially the new Google Base) may be a bigger marketplace than eBay. Read more in Chapter 4.

All this is just a forewarning that you will see references to Froogle, Craig's List, and other online marketplaces from time to time in this book. And, yes, they are relevant to your eBay retail business.

Summary

This chapter outlines some essential considerations you need to use in picking products with which to establish your eBay retail business. This will get you off to a good start whether your business is still in the conceptual stage or whether you have an existing business to which you would like to add additional product lines. Chapter 27 can also help you choose products.

Once you determine which products you want to sell, you can look at the sources of products starting with Chapter 9 to actually find wholesalers and other suppliers where you can acquire the products.

Before you plunge in, however, you will want to test the waters; that is, you will want to research the market for whatever inventory you choose to sell (see Chapter 27). And you will want to make sure that the products you choose to sell fit your personal situation and support your aspirations (see Chapter 3).

All things considered, this book will help you to identify, choose, and find inventory the smart way to sell on eBay.

2

Cost-Effectiveness

As we mentioned in the last chapter, cost-effectiveness is something you must always keep in mind as an eBay retailer, whether in regard to your shipping operation, software maintenance, other business operations, or in this case finding, acquiring, and carrying inventory. Cost-effectiveness does not have to do with just money. It has to do with resources. Resources include your money, time, employees' time, or subcontractor's time. Cost-effectiveness also includes the difficulty of handling products, because difficulty usually leads to additional time spent in handling.

Costs

You need to assess the various costs of carrying a product in your inventory to determine whether you can carry it cost-effectively.

Handling

Suppose the product gets delivered in bulk from your wholesaler in a large package filled with non-reusable packing materials. You will have to unpack that large carton, remove the unpackaged products, and dispose of the packing materials (which you cannot use again).

Next you will have to package each individual product for shipping to your future customers. That's a lot of handling.

For instance, in addition to putting the product in a package for shipping, you may also have to put it in a merchandising package. Hence, you might want to put a ruby bracelet (that you received in bulk packaged in an individual plastic bag) in a nice jewelry display box before you put it in another box intended for shipping. All this time and effort adds up, and this is a factor in whether you can handle the product in a profitable way.

On the other hand, if a wholesaler ships a bulk shipment of products in merchandising boxes already packed in shipping boxes, that's a benefit. All you have to do is open the top of the shipping carton, pull out the products one by one, and put a shipping label on them.

Packaging

As we've already hinted in the example above, the cost of packaging is a significant consideration also. Often you will need to repackage products for subsequent shipment to your customers. And the repackaging may entail two packages. A nice merchandising package is always appropriate, and a shipping package is always required. In addition to the time and effort required to handle the products, you need to consider the cost of packaging materials.

You will need to consider the cost of the packaging on behalf of your customers who will pay for it (as part of shipping and handling). Then, too, where you include shipping and handling (and therefore packaging) as part of the purchase price, the cost of packaging becomes an expense for you.

In addition, in some cases you may have to pay for packaging for shipments from your wholesaler.

Shipping

Shipping is directly relevant to cost-effectiveness. You pay to have inventory shipped to you. In some cases, you pay to ship products to your customers (when shipping and handling is included in the purchase price). This is covered more fully in Chapter 6.

Storage

If you are to keep products on hand after being received from a manufacturer or wholesaler before you in turn sell them to consumers, you will have to store them. Storage can be a minor expense or a major expense.

Short Time

Let's first consider it as a minor expense. You receive the products, store them in your garage, sell them on eBay, and send them to your customers all within a period of two weeks. The beauty of an eBay business is that this is entirely possible. You can anticipate when you are going to receive your inventory and you can set up your auctions so that you sell your products in a very short time.

This is called quick turnover. You can turn over your products in an eBay retail business much quicker than you normally can in a retail store offline.

Unfortunately, it depends on your supplier as to whether you can do this effectively. If your supplier ships quickly and is reliable, it's entirely possible. If your supplier is unreliable and ships at irregular intervals after you have put in an order, you have no choice except to store the products for a much longer time (or get a new supplier).

Long Time

Let's take a look at the more expensive cost of handling inventory. As we have hinted already, it will cost you more to store your products for a longer time because you will need more space. Space costs money (i.e., rent). This may not be a factor if you are using your garage and have enough space, which you consider to be "free." But when you outgrow your garage and need to rent warehouse space to store your products, it will suddenly occur to you that storage costs money and that storing certain products costs more money than storing other products. Thus, storage becomes a consideration that you need to make when choosing a product. The cost of storage makes selling the product less cost-effective. It could turn out that the cost of storage diminishes profitability too much.

Shrinkage

The volume of stored merchandise often shrinks. It is eaten by vermin, damaged by movement, stolen by employees, or reduced by any one of a number of other shrinkage factors. This is a cost of storage too.

Security

You need to take security measures to protect your stored inventory. Perhaps in your garage this isn't a problem. Perhaps in a warehouse security is provided and covered by the rent. If not, it may become an another cost of storage.

Insurance

Inventory consists of valuable merchandise, assets that require insurance to cover your risk of loss (e.g., fire, rain, and theft). This, like rent, is another cost of carrying inventory.

Interest

There is an additional factor here that adds to the cost of storage. That's the cost of carrying your inventory. This simply means that if you turn your inventory over quickly, you don't need a lot of capital for inventory. Indeed, if you can sell the inventory to your retail customers before you have to pay the wholesaler for it, you require no capital at all for inventory. The inventory will cost you nothing to carry. And with good credit and a long history of paying on time, you may be able to pull that off.

A more normal situation, however, is that you will have to pay for your inventory up front or before it is completely sold. The longer the turnover time, the more money you will need (i.e., the more capital you will need to carry your inventory). A greater amount of capital means borrowing more money (in most cases). And that means you will pay more interest (the cost of capital).

Again, this is an important consideration that you will want to make in the process of choosing products suitable for cost-effective and profitable sales.

Planning

Planning when you order inventory will keep your costs under control. Here are some guidelines:

- Stagger your orders where possible. Rather than one big order (requiring more storage) to hold you over for a long time, order your inventory more often to hold you for shorter periods. You need to balance this technique with the need to put in large orders to get volume discounts and the extra administrative cost of submitting staggered (multiple) orders.

- Anticipate sales and tailor your inventory orders to your future sales. Keep track and know at what point your inventory will be so low that you need to reorder so as to never be out of stock.

- Use triggers to help you remember to reorder. Triggers are automatic reminders to reorder when inventory gets too low.

- Don't cut it too close. Give yourself a buffer, that is, some extra time to get your inventory. Order a little earlier than you need to. This will result in more inventory on hand than you need to satisfy you customers; but look at it as an insurance policy against disappointing buyers and possibly getting negative feedback.

- Keep your eye on the goal. You want to turn over your inventory as often as possible while still always having a little more inventory on hand than you need.

- Use auction mangement software to manage your inventory. A good inventory management software module will provide you with the management capability, including triggers, to control your inventory cost-effectively.

Product Profit Model

As we mentioned in Chapter 1, you will also want to apply the product profit model to the products you are considering for retail sales in order to determine whether the costs inherent in that model will disqualify the products you intend to sell. Chapter 3 covers the product profit model.

Drop Shipping

The most cost-effective way to manage shipping and handling seems to be drop shipping. Drop shipping is where you just take the orders and then pass the orders on to a wholesaler or manufacturer who actually ships the products to your customers. This seems like the ideal situation, and it often is because you don't have to do any shipping or handling at all.

Is this always cost-effective? Not necessarily. If the drop shipper charges too much, it may be more cost-effective for you to receive, handle, store, and ship the product yourself.

It all boils down to a matter of cost. How can you tell how much the drop shipping costs? Compare the wholesale prices of the product from the drop shipper to the prices of suppliers that do not drop ship. Thus, you will be able to accurately estimate the additional cost of the drop shipping. We cover drop shipping thoroughly in Chapter 7 because it can be a substantial opportunity for you to handle your products cost-effectively. Consequently, we will not explain it more fully here.

Middlemen

Eliminate middlemen where possible, particularly where they don't contribute value to the chain of supply. If you can buy for less, you increase the cost-effectiveness of your inventory acquisition activities. Each person or business between you and the manufacturer diminishes your profit.

For instance, suppose the product goes from the manufacturer to the wholesaler to the drop shipper to the drop shipping service to you. You've got three middlemen between you and the manufacturer. Each takes a percentage, and your cost to acquire the product goes up.

If you can, it makes sense to eliminate all middlemen so that it's just you and the manufacturer negotiating a deal to acquire some products. Keep your eyes open. Occasionally, you will find opportunities to get around one or another middleman. Grab such opportunities to lower your inventory acquisition costs.

Moreover, shy away from deals that seem to be loaded with an excess of middlemen. They may not be as good as they look. For instance, closeouts can be burdened with middlemen. For closeouts, you want to get close to the business doing the closeout, whether it be a retailer that wants to get rid of excess inventory or a supplier that wants to disgorge large lots from a warehouse. There tend to be several jobbers and brokers in between with each taking a percentage. Such a closeout may not provide you with a cost-effective purchase.

Of course where a middleman plays a crucial role, you may not want to get around it. If a manufacturer requires a minimum purchase of $50,000 for a coffee maker, you may be glad to deal with a wholesaler that requires a minimum purchase of only $500. Likewise, if you want to have a coffee maker drop shipped, you may be glad to deal with a drop-shipping service that aggregates its retailer-customers to buy in volume from a wholesaler.

Negotiation

Negotiate everything. Your purchases from suppliers aren't retail purchases with fixed consumer prices. They're commercial purchases. Everything is up for negotiation.

The first rule of negotiation is: ask. A successful and inspirational real estate guru, Dee Fountain, has said, "Ask not, and you shall receive not." It's amazing what you can get if you ask for it. Utterly amazing! That is not to say you will get everything you ask for. But just asking for something is a great negotiating technique that often works.

Obviously, a skillful and successful negotiation can make your purchases more cost-effective. Invest some time and money in honing your negotiating skills. Teaching negotiation skills is beyond the scope of this book, but there's no shortage of books on the topic.

What are some of the things you might negotiate? The following is a partial list:

- Free samples or a nominal price for samples (for quality evaluation or test marketing)

- Smaller quantities than the stated minimum

- Free shipping, a reduced shipping rate, or shipping with a less expensive shipper

- Lower prices
- Less expensive packaging
- 30-day credit
- You name it

The best way to deal with suppliers is (1) negotiate, (2) negotiate, and (3) negotiate.

Always keep in mind that negotiation is a never-ending process. For instance, as your eBay business increases its sales, your continuous negotiations with suppliers should get you lower and lower wholesale prices based on greater volume.

Summary

The ideas discussed in this chapter should become second nature to you once you are operating a retail business. If you're already operating a retail business, you will already be taking into account many of the considerations that we cover in this chapter. So we intend this chapter to be a good starting point for people just getting into an eBay retail business and a good refresher for those that are already selling at retail on eBay.

3

Product Profit Model

It's great to find an appealing product that might sell well. It's equally encouraging to discover that you can acquire the product at a lower cost from a specific supplier than you can sell it for on eBay. Unfortunately, intelligent analysis doesn't end there. First, you need to have a business plan for your eBay retail business (doesn't have to be formal) that satisfies your financial aspirations. Then you need to determine whether each product that you propose to sell fits into that operating plan. Make no mistake; the failure to calculate an accurate *product profit model* may lead you to make poor product decisions and impair your profitability as well as your satisfaction with your eBay business.

Using Numbers

Building a useful product profit model requires that you first determine your personal financial needs. That process is beyond the scope of this book, but *eBay Business the Smart Way,* Second Edition, covers it. Once you have established your personal financial needs accurately, it is easy to use that figure to calculate your product profit model. For the purposes of illustration in this chapter, we will assume that your financial needs add up to a specific dollar amount each year. The analysis of that dollar amount is irrelevant to the product profit model. The product profit model simply starts with a single figure (the result of analyzing your financial needs) that satisfies your annual personal financial aspirations.

To make comparative calculations use the following:

- 2000 work hours per year

- 50 work weeks per year (two weeks annual vacation)

- 250 work days per year

These numbers are not absolutely accurate, but they're close enough. They assume you work a 40-hour week.

Personal Finances

eBay Business the Smart Way, Second Edition, advises you to take into account the personnel benefits such as health insurance, dental insurance, contribution to a pension fund, and the like that you need to know in order to estimate the amount of profit that you need in order to to live off an eBay business. It's the result of such calculations you need to help you determine what products will help you achieve your financial goals. For the purposes of this discussion, let's say you need $40,000 per year to pay yourself and fund your benefits.

Other Considerations

Non-financial considerations are often personal. For instance, you may receive a product from a wholesaler that weighs five pounds. It probably won't bother you to receive the shipment, store the product in your garage, repack it, and take it to UPS (or take it to the front of your house for UPS to pick it up). But what about a product that weighs 20 pounds? 40 pounds? 80 pounds? 160 pounds? At some point, you will find the size and the weight of the product is unsuited to your personal aspirations. In other words, it's a product that you just don't care to handle.

For instance, if you have a bad back, you probably don't want to handle large or heavy items. If you have an uncle who owns a local trucking company, you may feel fine about selling large or heavy items (assuming you can handle them) because the family connection provides a competitive advantage for you. (Many eBay retailers shy away from large or heavy products that must be shipped by truck.)

If you love accounting, you may be willing to handle 40 items a day or even 140 items a day (with the help of software, of course). If you can't stand accounting, you may be willing to handle only five items a day.

If you are going to keep inventory on your premises, the size of your garage may place limitations on what kind of products you can carry.

Your working hours may limit what you do. Do you watch after the kids all day and start working only after your spouse gets home from a job in the evening?

You need to take all things into consideration in building a product profit model for the ideal product. (Read the Time section later in the chapter for thoughts about time requirements.) You begin by determining how much money you want to make per year. Then you decide how many items you can handle per day and under what circumstances. Then you can calculate how much profit you have to make per item.

The Ideal Product

The ideal product is defined as follows (see Figure 3.1):

> The ideal product is the one that makes the most profit per item for an acceptable amount of work and is within *your* notion of what type of handling is acceptable.

Some people will gladly ship and account for 40 items a day to make a profit of $160 ($40,000 per year). Others wouldn't get into an eBay business where they had to handle 40 items per day without making enough money to hire someone else to help. But how can you afford to hire someone else to help you on only $40,000 a year and still have enough left over to make a decent living?

Everyone is different and in different circumstances. Each product is different and requires a different degree of effort in marketing and handling. You have to decide what your product profit model is. It's not that you're going to be able to do business exclusively with products that fit your model. Business is not that simple. Nevertheless, your product profit model is something against which you can measure all the opportunities you come across for selling products on eBay.

Figure 3.1 The ideal product.

Commodity Products

Would you handle 40 pre-packaged, mass-produced items a day? All you have to do is paste a mailing label on them and have UPS pick them up. Of course you have to do the accounting for them too and work with a wholesaler to keep the inventory coming in. In addition, that's 200 auctions a week that you have to run on eBay. But this probably isn't too much. This is probably an attractive business for many people for $40,000 per year. You have to make $4 profit per product $(($40,000 \div 250) \div 40 = $4)$.

Overworked

Joe had a client who ran 400 eBay auctions a week without auction management software and additionally operated an offline retail store in which he worked everyday during business hours. This level of activity is not recommended for those who desire to stay sane or remain married.

Fortunately, Joe devised a database system (in the days before the availability of good auction management software) for the client to handle the eBay auctions. Via an eBay bulk listing, the system greatly reduced the amount of time required to post the auctions.

Unique Products

Would you handle 40 antiques (not commodity items) a day? You have to pack them for shipping and have UPS pick them up. You have to do the accounting for them. And you have to keep finding more to purchase for your inventory. In addition, you have to run 200 auctions a week. Antiques are unique and require communication with bidders that's more intensive than average.

This seems impossible for one person to do, and you might decide you wouldn't even attempt to do it alone for $40,000 per year. You would need to pay at least two people $25,000 a year each to help you, and you would want to make $40,000 a year yourself to manage such an operation. That requires an average profit of $9 per antique (($90,000 ÷ 250) ÷ 40 = $9).

Pickers

Note that you would need to use pickers (see Chapter 16) too, presumably increasing the cost of acquiring inventory.

This use of the product profit model for unique items is a little different than the use for a commodity item. For a commodity product, you calculate the product profit model once and it works for each product. Instead, for unique products, you have to calculate the product profit model for each product (theoretically).

Seems like a lot of work. Fortunately, you can make some general assumptions and use the product profit model efficiently for unique items too. Let's assume you do that accurately in the antique business. What does your analysis above tell you?

Does it tell you that you can't handle any antiques that generate a profit under $9?

Well, one approach might be to aim for an average of $9 profit per antique. Certainly some antiques will generate more than $9 profit. Therefore, you can sell other antiques for less than $9 profit and still sell (and handle) the same number of antiques per day.

Hence, the product profit model for your antique business provides you with a useful guide for your daily retail operation in regard to your financial aspirations. Indeed, perhaps you had the idea that you could sell little antique knickknacks on eBay for $10 or $15. The product profit model tells you that there's likely not to be enough profit in selling such items to achieve your financial goals.

Case Study

You need to make $40,000 a year but want to handle only five items a day. Each item can take more than an average amount of communication with bidders, but not a lot more. You're willing to order inventory, but you don't want to have to go looking for inventory. Finally, you want to work a 40-hour week.

You need to find products that you can order from a wholesaler and on which you can make an average profit per item of $32 (($40,000 ÷ 250) ÷ 5 = $32). This calculation gives you a guideline for decision making when considering inventory opportunities.

Another Slant on the Product Profit Model

The product profit model doesn't take into consideration passion. If you are passionate about the cell phone accessories business, for instance, then you might be better off pursuing that business regardless of the product profit model for two reasons. First, your passion will fuel your motivation, and you will be more likely to be successful. Second, cell phone accessories have a bright future.

Nevertheless, creating a product profit model, for cell phone accessories will help you better formulate how to operate profitably in that particular market niche.

Calculating the Profit

Calculating the profit on a product is simple yet complex. The idea is simple. You subtract from the sales price the cost of the product and the amount of overhead allocated to the product. The remainder is your profit. Unfortunately, sometimes estimating the amount of your overhead is complex (but not impossible). Here's a simple example:

Sales price	$83
Cost of product	$47
Direct cost to sell product	$5

Overhead allocated to product $10

Profit per product $21

Thus, your profit per product sold will be $21. This is an estimate only. You want to make it as accurate as possible, but it doesn't have to be accurate to the penny. You calculate it simply to give you an idea of whether the sale of a product will contribute adequately to your financial aspirations.

The Numbers

Where do you get the numbers for calculating the profit? Let's look at them one by one.

Sales Price

You determine the anticipated sales prices of various products by your research on eBay (i.e., in Completed Listings), other places online, and offline. See Chapter 27.

Cost of Product

You determine the cost of products by finding suppliers where you can acquire the products at a lower price than you can sell them for.

Direct Costs to Sell Product

You need to estimate the unique costs for each product that can be directly attributed to handling and selling it. If all your products are nearly the same with the same direct costs, you don't need to make this calculation; just include the direct costs in overhead.

However, when the direct costs are substantially different amounts for different products, it makes sense to separate them from general expenses (overhead). For instance, let's say you sell model sailing ships and parts. Your average eBay fee to sell a model ship is $14. Your average eBay fee to sell a part is $1.15. This is a case where the eBay fees should be attributed directly to the products rather than added to overhead.

Overhead Allocated to Product

Your overhead is the sum of all business expenses except those you have separated out as direct costs to sell specific products.

How do you allocate the overhead? If all your products are nearly the same and require the same resources for handling, you can allocate the overhead evenly; that is, you can divide the total overhead by the total number of products sold to get an allocation amount per product.

When products are substantially different and require different resources for handling, your allocation becomes more complex if you do it intelligently. The idea is to make a reasonably accurate estimate of how much it costs to sell a product, and allocating overhead is part of the cost. These are the kinds of allocations that provide accountants with plenty of work and sometimes drive businesspeople mad. In other words, this is usually the most difficult part of the calculation.

Profit Per Product

When you subtract the cost of the product, the direct costs to sell the product, and the allocation of overhead to the product from the sales price of the product, you have calculated the profit per product. It is this number together with other information that will give you a good idea of whether you want the product in your retail inventory.

The Calculation Changes

When you grow, two things are likely to happen. Your overhead will increase because you will need more help both from people and possibly from additional software and equipment. You will then need to readjust the overhead component of your profit-per-item calculation to keep it accurate.

What About Your Current Sales Plan?

Suppose you're an expert on digital voice recorders, transcription, and creating audio records. You have a current plan to sell voice recorders and related software and equipment on eBay. You perceive that there's an untapped niche available and a growing market for such products. You don't need to do a product profit model, right? Actually, a profit model will give you a lot of insight into what you are doing or are about to do on eBay.

Should you create a product profit model for digital voice recorders, you might come to one of several different conclusions. Here are some possibilities:

1. Your business will be profitable and reasonably easy to manage well without an employee.

2. You should sell related software and equipment but not voice recorders.

3. You should sell voice recorders but not related software and equipment.

4. You should look for another niche on eBay.

5. Some other conclusion.

A product profit model is just another way of looking at the numbers in your business plan. And each different way you can look at the numbers will bring additional enlightenment.

Time

Shouldn't your product profit model consider time? Yes. It's assumed that you will estimate the time spent handling each product and include it in your evaluation when you consider the numbers. In fact, you might want to take a systematic approach and consider time methodically, even going so far as taking time measurements for the various handling tasks.

Remember that time is only a "free" resource so long as it is your time. If it's an employee's time, then you can put a dollar value on it. And time is always a limited resource, whether it's your time or an employee's time.

It's beyond the scope of this book to include time analysis calculations and systems. Nonetheless, be reminded that manufacturers, bureaucratic organizations, and service organizations have used time studies to cut costs and increase profits for over a century.

A time analysis for an offline retail store may not make as much sense. After all, customers stream in all day at different rates with different needs based on their own convenience, not yours. You have to handle whatever comes in the door every day. Some days you are busy and some days not, but you have to be there ready for customers in any event.

But an online retail business is different. It's more like a manufacturing operation. The orders come in. The packages go out. And then you (or your employees) go on to do some other work (perhaps even in some other place) without worrying about customers coming in the door to disrupt your efforts. Time studies, therefore, can be more meaningful.

Summary

Every successful retailer thinks about these concerns and includes them consciously or unconsciously in business decisions about inventory. Unfortunately, they often do this by winging it, which results in inaccuracies. We are simply advocating pursuing these concerns by considering them systematically.

The product profit model is a simple system that enables you to make calculations that will foster better business decisions regarding your choice of products to sell—products to include in your inventory. Use it. Put it down on paper (or in a word-processor document) for a product. Save it. Refer to it from time to time. Revise it. Use it to make decisions. In other words, don't wing it.

You will go through this process anyway, consciously or unconsciously. Might as well do it in a systematic way that will lead to greater profitability and greater satisfaction with your eBay retail business.

4

Inventory Management Software

If you're serious about being an eBay retailer, you need to get organized in the most cost-efficient way possible. That means using an
auction management service or program suite. It's inexpensive and
saves labor. It makes your job much easier. It even gives you valuable
reports on your business. It's hard to imagine operating an online
business without it.

A typical service or suite of programs enables you to do efficiently one
of your most important tasks: manage your inventory. Without careful
inventory management, your accounting will be inaccurate, and you
will lose track of how you are doing financially. Moreover, without
accurate inventory management you will disappoint a buyer sooner or
later—most likely sooner. That leads to negative feedback, something
that no eBay seller can afford.

Auction Management Software

Virtually all auction management software programs include an
inventory management function. There are dozens and dozens of
auction management software services available. Some work via the
Web, and some work on your desktop PC. Many of them provide you

with a whole range of functions that enable you to manage your eBay retail business digitally, a very cost-effective capability.

Auction management software is not expensive and can take the place of several employees. It can also provide the information you need in your business to make good business decisions. That is, many auction management services provide you with comprehensive reports that will give you a good idea of how successful you are and indicate changes that you might make for greater profitability.

However, it all starts with inventory management. You do not want to use an auction management service that does not provide you with comprehensive inventory management.

Competitive Advantage

By managing your inventory properly, you can cut costs and operate your eBay retail business more cost-effectively. That will give you an advantage over your competitors that do not use such software. On the other hand, if you do not use such software, you are at a disadvantage to your competitors that do use the software to manage their eBay retail businesses. Although acquiring inventory to sell on eBay is an important activity, it's just as important to manage your inventory well once you have acquired it. eBay gives you a fantastic opportunity to turn your inventory over quickly, something that few offline retailers are able to do. The best way to take advantage of this opportunity is to get serious about actively managing your inventory.

Datafeed Marketing

An inventory management program is essentially a database. The database holds all the information on your inventory; when you ask it to, it sends that data to eBay to fill (populate) your auction listings with text and photographs.

Of course, this is all behind the scenes. All you see when you use inventory management software is your inventory as a list or table of items. You decide what will be auctioned on eBay or be offered for sale in an eBay Store by clicking on items in your inventory list.

Keep in mind that this is your data. Your data either resides in your desktop PC, or in the case of an Internet auction management service, it resides on the computer used by the service. In other words, you never give away your data to eBay. You just send a *copy* of your data to eBay when necessary to create auction listings or eBay Store listings.

Well, how about sending that data to another marketplace? If you list your products in another marketplace, you will increase your chances of making a sale. That's called sending a datafeed, which is then used by the other marketplace to fill its catalog pages with your inventory information.

Froogle, operated by Google, makes a good example. By sending a datafeed to Froogle, your selected products will appear in the Froogle catalog (online). Since Froogle does not charge you for having your products appear in its online product directory (catalog), this is a no-brainer for creating a considerable number of additional sales. (Google is the leading search engine with more than twice as much traffic as Yahoo.) And auction management software, in particular inventory management software, makes this very easy to do. This is called data-feed marketing, and you can read about it in more detail in *Building Your eBay Traffic the Smart Way.*

Note that with datafeed marketing there is always setup work that needs to be done before the datafeed will work. Some of that work is digital and some administrative. Your auction management service should take care of the digital setup, and you will need to make the arrangements to participate in the target marketplace.

You need inventory management software to enable you to take part in this new and profitable means of expanding your sales online. The one thing that such software needs to do—and you should make sure of this—is that once a product is sold, whether on eBay, Froogle, or wherever, the product must be removed from your inventory. That means that with each sale, your inventory count for that particular product will be reduced.

If you let the inventory of that product run out, you will need to prematurely close your eBay auctions for that item. Otherwise you may sell something on eBay that you don't have in inventory, making it possible that you will get negative feedback. Again, inventory management software should enable not only datafeeds to other online marketplaces, but also provide automation for closing auctions and removing products from marketplaces when the inventory for such products is reduced to zero.

If your inventory management software manages your inventory properly, however, you are unlikely to run out of product. The software will automatically order (or remind you to order) additional inventory far enough ahead so that you never run out.

Just-In-Time Inventory

Carrying inventory requires money (i.e., capital for rent and interest). With the quick turnover of inventory on the eBay, you may be able to avoid having to carry inventory for long periods. In fact, you may be able to sell the inventory before you pay for it. (See Chapter 2.)

When your inventory is delivered just in time to be sent out to the customers that buy it, it's called a just-in-time inventory system. If you strive to have a just-in-time inventory system, you can potentially increase your profitability because you minimize or eliminate your rent and interest expenses.

The auto companies are very good at doing this. They assemble autos in an assembly plant, and the parts are delivered just in time to be assembled into the autos. The inventory of parts needed to assemble cars at the assembly plant is measured in hours, not days. If you visit an assembly plant, you will see a lot of trucks coming and going.

The longest auction period on eBay is 10 days. Consequently, if you can have your inventory delivered in a just-in-time inventory operation, you should theoretically not have to carry it more than 10 days.

Anticipation

To set up a just-in-time inventory operation, you must first anticipate your sales. Then you must determine how long it takes from when you order the products from the supplier until the products arrive at your location. You order far enough in advance so that the inventory arrives just in time to send to customers. Of course, you might build in a cushion of a few days just in case something goes wrong—which it will occasionally.

Note that it takes a reliable supplier to make a just-in-time inventory system work well. You have to be able to count on timely deliveries.

A just-in-time inventory system is something to strive for. It will not be easy to set up, but once set up, it should be easy to operate. Only auction management software will enable you to set it up and make it work well.

Resources

Below is a partial list of the Web auction management services available. Survey them to see what each offers in the way of inventory management (and research capability):

Andale, *http://www.andale.com*

AuctionHawk, *http://www.auctionhawk.com*

AuctionHelper, *http://www.auctionhelper.com*

Auctiva, *http://auctiva.com*

AuktionMaster, *http://auktionmaster.net*

ChannelAdvisor, *http://channeladvisor.com*

DEK Auction Manager, *http://dekauctionmanager.com*

HammerTap Manager, *http://www.hammertap.com*

Kyozou, *http://kyozou.com*

ManageAuctions, *http://www.manageauctions.com*

Marketworks, *http://auctionworks.com*

Meridian, *http://www.noblespirit.com*

Mpire, *http://www.mpire.com*

InkFrog, *http://www.inkfrog.com*

Truition, *http://truition.com*

Vendio, *http://www.vendio.com*

Zoovy, *http://zoovy.com*

Today, it is difficult to distinguish between programming delivered on the Web and programs that work from your computer. Auction management services provide programming via the Web but also provide certain programs that work from your desktop computer for selected functions. On the other hand, most desktop auction management programs reside on your computer but perform certain functions via the Internet from a remote server (see Figure 4.1). Each year, the distinctions get more obscure.

Check out the following if you prefer desktop programs over Web programming services:

AuctionMessenger, *http://www.auctionmessenger.net*

AuctionTamer, *http://www.auctiontamer.com*

Auction Wizard 2000, *http://www.auctionwizard2000.com*

Blackmagik utilities (for Mac), *http://blackmagik.com*

Cricketsniper, *http://cricketsniper.com*

CoreSense, *http://coresense.com*

EZLister, *http://www.ezlister.net*

Infopia, *http://www.infopia.com*

MarketBlast, *http://marketblast.com*

ShootingStar, *http://www.foodogsoftware.com*

Timber Creek Sold, *http://www.timbercreeksoftware.com*

SpoonFeeder, *http://spoonfeeder.com*

YukonSoft, *http://yukonsoft.com*

Read more about auction management services and software in *eBay Business the Smart Way,* Second Edition.

And don't forget eBay's auction management software, Turbo Lister (free – see Figure 4.2), Selling Manager, Selling Manager Pro, File Exchange, and Blackthorne, together with eBay Sales Reports. You can find them on eBay. Go Sell, Seller Central, Seller Tools. Also look for the eBay Solutions Directory link under Third-Party Services at Seller Central.

Figure 4.1 MarketBlast website. ©1995-2005 4D, Inc.

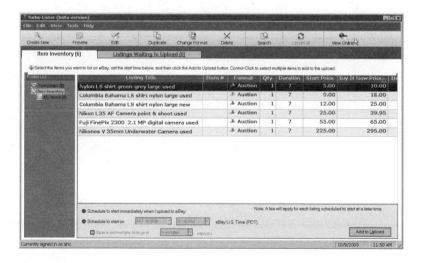

Figure 4.2 eBay's Turbo Lister, a basic way to keep track of inventory.

Summary

An auction management service or software package is a must to retain sanity and maintain efficiency. In particular, a valuable component is inventory management software. Using it will not only keep you out of trouble with your customers (e.g., by not selling inventory you don't have) but will also potentially increase profitability with just-in-time inventory management and open retailing opportunities such as datafeed marketing.

II

The Basics

5

Supplier-Retailer Relationships

The very basis of retail knowledge is to understand the chain of supplier-retailer relationships and where you fit in. The goal in regard to any product is to find the supplier relationship that gives you the largest margin of profit and the greatest reliability. This chapter provides you with the background information necessary to analyze every offering you come across in order to understand whether you're getting the best deal you can. The alternative is to seek a better offer elsewhere, and often you have to do so. Because there is such a variation in supplier-retailer relations—particularly in margins—across many industries, you will have to take this general knowledge and apply it to your situation. For surely if you do not become adept at maximizing your profit margins, you will never realize your full financial potential.

Chain of Relationships

There is a chain of relationships starting with the manufacturer and ending with the retailer.

Direct Sales

Many manufacturers sell directly to retailers (and some even to consumers). They simply have an open policy that they will sell to any wholesaler or retailer. And they sell in any quantity ordered. Thus, many retailers will purchase inventory direct. Some wholesalers will also purchase such inventory. (There are always retailers that never order direct from manufacturers, and some wholesalers will service those types of retailers.)

Times Are Changing

Advances in digital and network technology enable more and more manufacturers to sell directly. That's a favorable trend for retailers. If manufacturers also sell directly to consumers, however, they become your competitors.

In order to sell direct, however, a manufacturer has to have a wholesale staff. Most manufacturers like doing what they do best: manufacturing. That's where they put their capital. Hence, they leave distribution up to the wholesalers.

Wholesaler Sales

A wholesaler is a business that orders large numbers of products from a manufacturer, stores the products, and sells (and ships) the products in smaller quantities to retailers. In other words, a wholesaler is also known as a *distributor.*

For example, a wholesaler may receive and store 100 cases of a product packed 12 to the case. In turn, the wholesaler sells the product to retailers in minimum quantities of one case (12 items). The wholesaler just reships the case in which the products arrived. There is no repackaging. For this distribution, the retailer pays the lowest wholesale price. If the wholesaler were to sell to retailers in smaller quantities, it would have to break a case and repackage the products, a process that costs money. Therefore, the retailer would have to pay a higher wholesale price.

Most manufacturers deal exclusively through wholesalers. This is the predominant relationship, particularly for smaller manufacturers. Under this arrangement, a wholesaler may get an exclusive territory. Depending on where you are located, you will buy from a designated wholesaler. In this case, you have no choice except to buy from a wholesaler, and you will not be permitted to buy directly from the manufacturer.

Wholesalers are not necessarily passive businesses that wait for the business to come to them. Many have a sales force which goes out and calls on its retail customers. Once you've established contact with a wholesaler, you may find yourself getting visited someday by a salesperson from the wholesaler.

Tip for the Novice

Your sales tax license is your passport to the world of wholesale. Trade shows and trade marts may not admit you without one, and suppliers won't sell to you without one. Getting one is the start of your search for inventory.

Most state websites are *http://www.XX.gov*, where XX is the two-letter code for the state (e.g., *http://www.ne.gov* for Nebraska – see Figure 5.1). Your state's website will give you a good start on tracking down the sales tax license information.

Dual Sales

Many manufacturers will sell to both wholesalers and retailers, but only in large quantities. Therefore, unless you are willing to purchase products in the minimum quantity set by the manufacturer, you will need to acquire the products through a wholesaler.

In a situation where a manufacturer will sell to anyone who orders the minimum quantity, there's less likely to be exclusive territories for wholesalers. That means you can shop around between the wholesalers to see who offers the best deals. You may not be forced to deal with a wholesaler in your geographical area.

Like many business arrangements, the manufacturer-wholesaler-retailer relationship can be simple or complex. It depends on many factors, and knowing the typical arrangements will help you understand the particular arrangements in your industry.

Retail Sales

A retailer is a retail business that normally buys merchandise from a wholesaler in small quantities and sells the products one at a time to consumers.

Consumers

Let's not forget consumers. They are the buyers, the people who buy products from retailers and use them.

Manufacturer's Reps

When manufacturers sell directly to retailers, they often use manufacturer's reps. The normal purpose of the manufacturer's reps is to call on customers (mostly retailers) and subsequently service those customers. Consequently, if you contact a manufacturer that works this way, you will find yourself being visited by a manufacturer's rep. The manufacturer's rep might be somebody on salary with a firm that represents manufacturers, or it might be a freelance manufacturer's rep (i.e., one person).

For instance, if you go to a trade show and make contact with a manufacturer, the representatives of the manufacturer at the trade show may be the manufacturer's reps or, if not, they may tell you that a manufacturer's rep will call on you.

The problem here is that if you're in a hurry to get inventory, having a manufacturer's rep call on you a month from now or six months from now may not do you much good. So you always want to get the name of the particular manufacturer's rep that will call on you, including the person's address, telephone number and email address. By comunicating immediately with the rep, you may be able to hurry the process of getting inventory.

A manufacturer's rep is like a wholesaler, except a rep stores no inventory, gets paid a commission, and charges a little less than the typical wholesale price.

Once you buy from the manufacturer, it's the manufacturer's rep who will service your account and iron out any problems you have. It's also the manufacturer's rep who will be an intermediary in communication between you and the manufacturer. The manufacturer has a manufacturer's rep specifically because they do not want to service your account or communicate directly.

Economics

The typical manufacturer-wholesaler-retailer relationship also has a typical scheme (suggested by the manufacturer) of splitting up the proceeds of the sale of a product. The following is a common model of the distribution of the sales price:

Business	Share of Sales Price
Manufacturer	50 percent
Wholesaler	10 percent
Retailer	40 percent

For example, let's say a product sells to a consumer for $100. The manufacturer gets $50, the wholesaler gets $10, and the retailer gets $40.

The price of the product to the wholesaler is $50. This is a discount from the wholesale price. The price of the product to the retailer is $60. This is the wholesale price. The price the consumer pays the retailer is $100. This is the full retail price also known as the retail list price or the manufacturer's suggested retail price (MSRP).

Markup

Now let's look at the economic position of the retailer. What's the markup in the typical example? It is 67 percent ($40 ÷ $60 = 0.67). The wholesale price is $60. The retail sales price is $100. The difference of $40 is the markup and is 67 percent of the *wholesale price*.

What if the wholesale price is $50, and the retail sales price is $100? What's the markup? It's 100 percent ($50 ÷ $50 = 1.00). This is called a *keystone* markup.

Margin

The margin is a different mathematical expression from a markup. What's the margin in the typical example? It is 40 percent ($40 ÷ $100 = 0.40). The wholesale price is $60. The retail sales price is $100. The difference of $40 is the margin and is 40 percent of the *sales price*.

To avoid confusion in this book, we pick only one mathematical expression to use, and that's the margin. It directly informs you what portion of the sales price of a product belongs to you. The margin is also the gross profit on the sale of the item.

Fat Margins

Fat margins bring a smile to an eBay retailer's face. That's the goal of your inventory purchasing process: to get the highest margins you can.

How High?

How high can your margin go on a product? Very high. The rule of thumb for mail-order success is that you can't make a decent profit without an 80 percent margin (500 percent markup). For example, if you bought an item for $10, you would have to sell it for $50. There are reasons for this that are beyond the scope of this book because it isn't a book about mail order. But this is a sharp deviation from the typical economic model set forth above. Yet such margins are not uncommon, particularly for non-name-brand products. It all gets down to the fact that every product is different. And there are millions of different products listed on eBay.

Lean Margins

Unfortunately, many eBay items don't sell for full retail price (i.e., list price or MSRP). The competition between retailers is often intense, and prices are forced lower. You are more likely to sell name-brand merchandise for a 10 percent margin (i.e., at a discount) on eBay than a 40 percent margin (i.e., at full retail).

Complicating Factors

Suppose the economic model above is the standard. (It's not, because there is no standard.) You will note that each business has its own margin. The retailer has a 40 percent margin, the wholesaler has a 10 percent margin, and the manufacturer has a 50 percent margin.

The manufacturer normally controls and publishes the suggested margins. Suppose the manufacturer decides that its margin for a product will be only 40 percent. Why would a manufacturer do that? Undoubtedly to be more competitive. The manufacturer might create a keystone margin (larger margin) for the wholesaler in an effort to get the wholesaler to carry more of the manufacturer's product and less of the competition's products.

Where's the Keystone?

The wholesaler may pass along the keystone margin to retailers, in which case the retailers will have keystone margins. But the wholesaler might keep the keystone margin to itself. Market conditions will dictate what the wholesaler will do.

Keep in mind that the suggested margins are not binding. The manufacturer can change its prices on a whim but cannot necessarily control what wholesalers or retailers charge. The wholesaler can sell for whatever wholesale price it can get away with. And the retailer will sell for whatever price it needs to in order to be competitive. The market is dynamic, and manufacturers' prices, wholesalers' prices, and retailers' prices change.

Nice to Know

It's at least nice to know the manufacturer's suggested wholesale price. Paying more than this price to a wholesaler for your inventory is probably unnecessary. Paying less is sometimes possible.

Let's look at typical practices that might change the margins in the typical economic model above.

Manufacturer

Most manufacturers offer different prices based on volume. A wholesaler that buys 1,000 products will pay a higher price per product than another wholesaler that buys 20,000 products. Buying in volume is invariably cheaper.

Manufacturers have closeouts. At the end of the 2006 season, a manufacturer might cut prices on 2006 products by 20 percent so that it can make way for sales on its 2007 products.

Wholesaler

A wholesaler is not bound by the manufacturer's suggested margins. Most wholesalers offer different wholesale prices based on volume. A retailer that buys 12 products will pay a higher price per product than another retailer that buys 144 products. Buying in volume is always cheaper.

In fact, the wholesale price for the purchase of just one item might be very close to the full retail price. In other words, the margin expands and shrinks depending on the volume of the purchase.

Do wholesalers have to pass along the closeout prices of a manufacturer? Not necessarily. But wholesalers want to move product as much as manufacturers and sometimes have excess inventory too. They even have their own closeouts to get rid of such excesses.

Retailer

A retailer is not bound by the manufacturer's suggested retail price either. Many retailers sell products today at discounts from full retail prices. Retailers can also buy closeouts from manufacturers, wholesalers, jobbers, and brokers and then undercut prevailing discount retail prices.

What It All Means

You can start out with a typical economic model that's simple and looks real. Yet add a few twists based on volume purchasing, and the model doesn't hold up. Throw in some closeouts, jobbers, brokers, and drop shippers, and the wholesale prices are all over the place. And we haven't even talked about myriad other factors that affect pricing at every level.

Alas, it's all very complicated. But what a great milieu for negotiating. The commercial world is dynamic. Negotiate everything.

The Wholesale Price

The price retailers pay to a manufacturer or wholesaler for a product is the wholesale price. Is the wholesale price always the same for the product? Clearly not. Read above.

If you can buy directly from a manufacturer (not possible with most manufacturers), the wholesale price may be a little lower than buying from a wholesaler, but the purchase may require a high-volume order.

Then there are drop shippers (see Chapter 7). The wholesale price drop shippers will charge you is the highest. They sell to you one product at a time (the lowest possible volume), and in addition, ship the products to your buyers for you.

As a retailer, your diligent research will quickly lead you to how much you have to pay to acquire a certain product for your inventory. There are no secrets if you do your homework.

In Certain Industries

In certain industries such as sporting goods and designer clothes, practice dictates that all retailers sell at MSRP. You will not find this requirement expressed in writing. These are usually industries tightly controlled by manufacturers where you are more likely to buy from a manufacturer's rep than a wholesaler.

If you are a discount retailer, you will not be permitted to become a dealer. If you become a buyer or dealer and afterwards sell the products at discount, you will find your relationship with the manufacturer terminated. Although this is a violation of the antitrust laws, the manufacturer will always find a reason to terminate the relationship for something other than discount pricing. Again, these pricing practices are limited to a few industries.

An advertising agreement—minimum advertised price (MAP)—may limit the prices at which you can advertise products in some industries. You will want to make sure you comply with MAP agreements, which may require being careful in how you write your eBay auction ads.

Your Competitor's Price

Can a competing retailer's retail price be lower than your wholesale price? Sure! Using the economic model above, suppose your competitor buys the minimum quantity (24 products) from the wholesaler on a product that sells for $100 at full retail price. Your competitor has a 40 percent margin and presumably can sell anywhere within that margin. Let's say she sells the product regularly on eBay for $70, a 30 percent discount off the full retail price. She makes $10 on every sale, as her wholesale price is $60. That's not a lot, but let's say it's enough to keep her eBay business humming along.

You can't buy the products 24 at a time (for whatever reasons). You use a drop shipper that charges you $75 (plus shipping) for each product you buy, one at a time. That's probably fair. Only by buying in minimum quantities do you get the normal wholesale price. Buying one at a time gets you the highest wholesale price. Hence, you buy at $75.

You can easily see that your wholesale price is $5 higher than her retail price. But that's not all. Let's say you have to have to sell the product for $85 to make a modest profit. Your retail price is $15 higher than her retail price. This does not bode well for the success of your business.

Beginnings

Get set up as a business before you approach any suppliers. You should have all of the following:

- Business name (optional but preferable to personal name)
- Sales tax license (see Figure 5.1)
- Tax ID number
- Telephone number
- Fax number
- Email address
- Custom-printed basic commercial forms (e.g., purchase orders)
- Business cards
- Letterhead stationery
- Physical address (not a PO box)
- Business shipping account (e.g., FedEx)
- Commercial bank account (checking)
- Financial statement
- Merchant credit card account (or PayPal)
- Business credit card (for quick payment)

You don't know when you might need any one of the above to do business immediately with a supplier, a vendor, a lender, or a customer. So make sure you have them all in place before you try to acquire inventory. The above checklist is also great for trade shows.

Partnerships

Manufacturer-retailer or wholesaler-retailer relationships when operating well should look like partnerships rather than run-of-the-mill business relationships. The objective is to sell products to consumers. As an eBay retailer, that is your job. And it's an important job, because if products don't sell to consumers, nothing happens. That's why retailers get paid so much for selling products. After all, a 40 or 50 percent margin, which is normal, is a substantial percentage of the price of the product to a consumer. So, manufacturers and wholesalers need you.

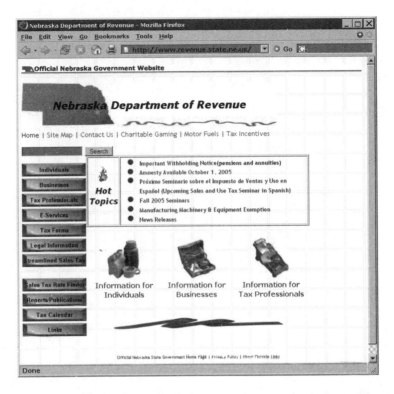

Figure 5.1 The Nebraska website (Department of Revenue), a good place to start looking for the requirements to get a sales tax license in Nebraska.

Likewise, you need manufacturers and wholesalers. Without them you would have nothing to sell. If you don't sell anything, you don't make a profit. Not only do you need inventory, but you need that inventory to be delivered safely (without damage in transport) and on time. Without such good service, it is often difficult to provide good customer service to your retail customers.

Consequently, the relationship should always be one of cooperation and never an adversarial one. It is very important for you to treat your suppliers well and avoid getting into a situation where you alienate them or treat them without respect. If you are dealing with suppliers that do not provide that kind of relationship for you, switch suppliers. Switch to suppliers that are supportive and with which you can achieve a just-in-time inventory system. (See Chapter 4 for more on just-in-time inventory systems.)

Just Once

If you sell the same merchandise on an ongoing basis, the advice above is good advice. If you deal with a supplier just once to sell a certain product for a short period and then move on to other products supplied by other suppliers, the advice above is still good advice. Why? First, you never know when you might have to deal with that supplier again. Second, it's more productive to have cooperative relationships and more pleasant too. Third, your professional reputation is at stake. Fourth, the retail business can be great fun when you have good relationships with your suppliers.

Dealer Status

Almost invariably you will want to achieve dealer status with the businesses that supply your inventory. It is not unusual for you to be able to acquire inventory and sell it without becoming a dealer. But being a dealer provides additional benefits such as:

- Preferential service
- Listed as dealer on manufacturer's website
- Getting lower prices from wholesalers
- Use of manufacturer's logo and advertising materials

Being a dealer is usually a good deal for you. But be sure to look at a supplier's requirements for becoming a dealer so that you know what you're getting into.

One of the benefits you might achieve with dealer status is exclusivity. By virtue of being a dealer, you will be the exclusive dealer within a certain local geographical area. As markets are no longer defined just by geography, you might be able to get an exclusive arrangement to sell the supplier's products on eBay or online. There may be restrictions that come along with the benefits. For instance, a dealership to sell a line of elegant clothing of a certain brand name may come with the restriction that you do not sell merchandise in your retail business that is below a certain quality. Sometimes these restrictions are not in writing. They are just understood in the industry.

Expect a manufacturer's general policies and dealership policies to be upheld by its wholesalers. Some manufacturers are very touchy about how their products are sold. They hold their distributors accountable for making sure retailers support such policies.

Never in Writing

Sometimes it's difficult to understand what's going on without asking a lot of questions. The antitrust laws affect many aspects of retailing. In an attempt to work around the edges of antitrust issues, suppliers sometimes have policies that they never express in writing.

Being a dealer also gives you credibility. Many manufacturers even provide special logos for official dealers to use. That shows that you're not selling products on the black market, gray market, or acquired from other unreputable sources. It gives consumers more confidence in dealing with you.

Physical Presence

In order to carry the products of some suppliers, you will have to have an offline store. They will refuse to deal with you if you are strictly an online business. In that case, it may be well worth your while to open a store in your community.

Joe knows a retailer who sells home theaters on eBay and does a huge volume. However, he cannot get inventory from the big name-brand manufacturers without having a physical store. So he operates a small store in his town in which he sells about 10 percent of his inventory. The other 90 percent he sells on eBay. If you're having trouble getting name-brand goods to sell in your retail business, opening a token store in your community may be the best path to selling first-class merchandise on eBay.

Financing Inventory

In *eBay Business the Smart Way,* Second Edition, financing inventory and getting bank loans are covered in detail. Here we will just mention that the ideal situation is for the supplier to finance your inventory for you. Ten-, fifteen-, and thirty-day financing is quite common if you can establish good commercial credit.

As we mentioned in Chapter 4 regarding a just-in-time inventory system, you should be able to turn over your eBay inventory very quickly. After all, the longest auction is 10 days. If you can sell your merchandise, get paid, and do it within 10 days, a manufacturer or wholesaler that gives you 15 days to pay for such inventory will, in effect, finance your inventory for you. That's why a just-in-time inventory system is so valuable. It reduces the need for capital to run your business. Keep in mind, however, that in order to get such good credit from your suppliers, you will need to have a good track record and maintain a good credit rating.

You will want to establish credit with your wholesalers and manufacturers early on. If you can get credit immediately for the small quantities you will need to get your business started, it will be much easier to get credit for the large quantities of inventory you will need later on as your business grows.

Whatever you do, once you have established credit with a supplier, always pay on time as agreed.

Co-Op Advertising

Co-op advertising is one of the useful benefits of having a good relationship with a supplier. A manufacturer or wholesaler may pay anywhere from 20 percent to 80 percent of the costs of your advertising for the products within certain limitations. For offline retailers, this is a prime benefit of which to take full advantage.

For online retailers, this benefit is not so obvious. If you use eBay exclusively for selling your products, advertising may not be important to you. However, even eBay offers you advertising opportunities with its keyword advertising program. Therefore, co-op advertising would presumably defray some of the expense of doing eBay keyword advertising.

In addition, if you sell in more than one market (for instance, on Froogle) as well as on eBay, you may feel the need to advertise. For instance, Google also offers keyword advertising (Google adwords). But you might even want to go beyond that and do some kind of banner advertising or other kind of online promotion. Therefore, co-op advertising offered by a supplier might be a good deal for you.

Customers

A poor supplier-retailer relationship is bound to have an adverse effect on your customers at some point. This needs to be avoided at all costs. Negative feedback can ruin your reputation. Rather, a good supplier-retailer relationship will be supportive of your customer service, and you will be able work out customer problems as quickly and efficiently as possible.

Summary

Your relationship with a supplier not only has a direct effect on your profitability, but it is also a mutually beneficial one that rewards mutual cooperation. Unfortunately, every supplier is different with different requirements and offering different benefits. There is no uniform template for a supplier-retailer relationship. It's up to you to take advantage of every benefit each supplier offers and meet every demand each supplier requires. If you can't establish a friendly and cooperative relatioship with a supplier, it may be time to move on. Sooner or later a bad relationship is bound to affect your buyers, a risk that you want to minimize. The good news is that there are thousands of suppliers ready to establish a healthy and productive relationship with you.

6

Shipping

Shipping works two ways. You receive the shipment (from the wholesaler) and have to pay for such shipping, and you send a shipment (to a customer) and may have to pay for it. Consequently, in evaluating a product, you need to pay attention to what it costs to ship the product in order to determine the burden on your profitability.

You pay to get your inventory to the place where you store it. You cannot assume this will be a nominal cost. This cost is, effectively, a part of your cost of goods, a figure that is used to calculate your profit. Some products cost a lot more to ship than other products, and when you are picking a product to sell, you need to be aware of the shipping cost to get the product to your location.

In many cases, you will charge the customer for the cost of sending the product to him or her. Thus, it's not your cost. Nonetheless, the cost of shipping affects the salability of the product. Then, too, where you include shipping and handling as part of the purchase price, you will pay for the shipping to customers. That becomes part of your cost of doing business.

FOB

FOB means *free on board*. It is followed by a place. It means that the merchandise you buy will be delivered at the place specified.

Thus, FOB Savannah means that for the price you are going to pay for the merchandise, it will be delivered at Savannah, Georgia.

If the factory is in Savannah and your place of business is in Springfield, Illinois, that means the merchandise you buy will be delivered at the loading dock of the factory in Savannah. You pay the freight from the factory to Springfield.

Wholesale to Retail Shipping

Inventory can be shipped from your supplier to you a number of ways from one product at a time to bulk shipments with hundreds of products. This shipping is something you don't want to leave to chance.

In some cases, you may not have a choice. The supplier ships a standard way and provides no choices. You pay the freight, so to speak. In other cases you have choices. There is no standard practice.

If you have accounts with the Postal Service, UPS, or FedEx and give permission to a supplier to use your account numbers, you may be able to create choices where none otherwise exist.

The object, of course, is to keep shipping costs down by having your inventory shipped to you the most cost-effective way. This means controlling—or at least understanding—how the products will be shipped and the cost of the shipping.

For example, bulk shipping by truck may cost $1.23 per product, a carton of six products shipped via UPS may cost $2.79 per product, while individual products shipped via UPS may cost $5.60 per product. If this is a product with a $35 sales price, controlling the shipping cost may be the most important thing you do to maximize profitability.

Just-In-Time Shipping

One of the great possibilities for an eBay retail business is quick inventory turnover. After all the sales period is 3, 5, 7, or 10 days. That's pretty quick for retail. You want to be sure to take advantage of this aspect of eBay selling to minimize your costs. For instance, with quick turnover you can avoid the following business requisites:

- Need for capital to carry a larger volume of inventory
- Need for storage space to store more inventory

Capital and storage both cost money (i.e., interest and rent). Consequently, you need to institute a just-in-time inventory system as Chapter 4 outlines. That means that you need to receive your inventory just in time to fill orders. This takes a high degree of organization and reliable suppliers (as covered in Chapter 4).

It also takes reliable shipping periods. To achieve reliable shipping periods requires controlling both the supplier and the shipper as much as possible.

Retail to Consumer Shipping Constraints

The shipping cost can be a touchy topic with eBay buyers. If it's included in the price, buyers don't worry about it. If buyers pay and the cost is reasonable, they accept it as part of shopping online. But they still figure it into the total cost of the item in regard to making a purchasing decision. If it's too much, they resent it and probably will not buy.

In light of the above, it's naive to think that the shipping cost doesn't matter. Even when it's not included in the purchase price, it's still part of the purchase price in the minds of buyers. They simply add it to the purchase price for purposes of comparative shopping.

The lesson to be learned here is that the shipping cost for your inventory does matter, even though the buyers pay it. It's an increase in the purchase price. If you've done your homework, you should know the highest probable price on eBay for each product you sell. That price includes the shipping cost.

For example, suppose you sell memory cards on eBay for digital cameras. The manufacturers charge consumers about $45 each (with free shipping). You can sell high-quality, third-party cards for $20 and make a reasonable profit Shipping costs buyers $1.06. Many consumers will be enticed to buy (if you can convince them the quality is OK) because their cost is $21.06 compared to $45.

But what if your competitors are selling similar memory cards for $12 on eBay? You decide to sell yours for $12 too but charge $8 for shipping and handling. Can you get away with it? We don't think so. Shipping costs do matter.

Resources

Here are some shipping resources where you can find further information:

DHL, *http://www.dhl-usa.com/index*

Federal Express, aka FedEx, *http://fedex.com/us* (see Figure 6.1)

Freightquote, *http://freightquote.com*

United Parcel Service, aka UPS, *http://ups.com*

US Postal Service, aka Post Office, *http://usps.com*

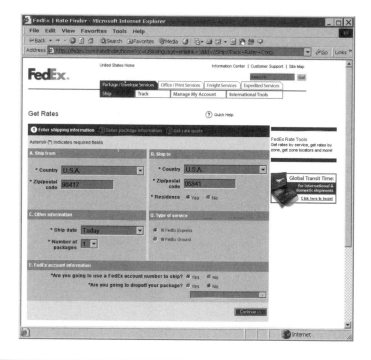

Figure 6.1 FedEx rate calculator webpage. ©1995-2005 FedEx. All rights reserved.

Summary

Routine shipping—from a supplier and to a customer—affects your bottom line and your marketing. You need to be vigilant. Hopefully, all shipping costs will be low. But sometimes they are not, particularly for low-priced items. Always take the shipping costs into account for both you and your customers.

7

Drop Shipping

When you order a product and the supplier ships it directly to your customer, not to you, that's drop shipping. Oh, the beauty of it! No fulfillment (packaging and shipping) operation. No storage. Just paperwork—or more accurately computer work. You sell the products on eBay, and the supplier ships them to your customers. It's the ultimate "inventoriless" retail business. Is it too good to be true?

No. It can work well for you if approached with intelligence and research, that is, the right information and the right suppliers. Drop shipping is definitely a technique that should draw your interest and warrant your serious consideration.

Advantages

For drop shipping, the manufacturer or wholesaler is the drop shipper. You are the stockless retailer or inventoriless retailer. Drop shipping has several powerful advantages that make it an attractive alternative to doing your own fulfillment.

Capital

You need no capital for carrying inventory and for setting up a fulfillment operation. You don't order the product (inventory) until a buyer pays for it. You use the buyer's money to acquire the product. The drop shipper ships it to the buyer.

Storage

Since you never take delivery of your inventory, you don't have to store anything. The drop shipper sends your inventory directly to buyers. That means you don't have to lease real estate or devote your garage to warehouse use.

Fulfillment

Neither do you have to run a fulfillment operation. Such an operation requires storage space, machinery, packaging, shipping supplies, digital shipping software, and perhaps personnel. It takes a few bucks to set it up so that it works efficiently. But it's not required for drop shipping, so you can save the capital for other purposes.

Fulfillment is a task for which many eBay businesses hire their first employee. It's tedious to do it yourself. Drop shipping eliminates the need for it. Thus, you can save yourself a lot of trouble as well as money.

Tracking

Many drop shippers provide you with a tracking number for each product shipped. You can pass the tracking number on to the buyer.

Returns

You don't have to replace product returns. That's the job of the drop shipping supplier.

Test-Market

You can test-market a product easily and inexpensively by selling just a few products without risk. If you have to buy in minimum quantities from wholesalers instead, you may have many items left over after a test-market effort proves an item can't be sold profitably on eBay.

Your Name

You don't necessarily give up your identity (your brand) when you drop ship. Professional drop shippers will put your name on the package so that your customers will think it is coming from you. Make sure this service is offered as part of your drop shipping arrangement.

Charge for Shipping and Handling

You can charge your buyers for shipping and handling to defray a portion of the drop shipping cost of handling and sending the products to them.

Disadvantages

Sorry to say that drop shipping isn't all advantages. There are some negatives you need to consider.

Never See It

When you acquire inventory from a drop shipper, you never see it. Who knows what your customers are getting? If you haven't seen samples of the exact products you sell, you're operating in the dark. This is risky. The best practice is to see what you're selling before you sell it.

Yet for name-brand merchandise, this risk is minimal. For instance, if you haven't seen a Sunbeam food blender, there is little risk in selling it. You rely on the brand to assure quality.

Control

Online retail sales have developed a reputation for quick delivery, assuming immediate payment (e.g., credit card, PayPal). eBay is no exception. If you don't deliver quickly after a customer has paid, you won't reach your optimal profitability. Your reputation won't let you. Therein lies the rub with drop shipping. You lose control over the fulfillment.

Consequently, you need reliable drop shippers that ship when they say they will ship and via such means that have a highly predictable transit period.

Suppose you use a drop shipper that will ship within 24 hours after your order is received via email. The drop shipper ships via FedEx Ground, which takes three days.

In this case, the auction ends, the buyer pays, and you immediately order the product from the drop shipper. This works well. The shipment is immediate to your customer. You can't order the drop shipping any sooner because you don't know who your buyer is until the end of the auction. You can advertise "Shipped within 24 hours."

But what if your drop shipper doesn't perform as represented? First, how will you know? If the product gets there seven days later instead of four days later, you will probably receive few complaints. But your customers won't think much of your delivery service. Second, what can you do about it? Will complaining solve the problem, or is the drop shipper a large bureaucratic organization that gives poor customer service (to you)? These are things to keep in mind when choosing a drop shipper.

Naturally, you will want some sort of verification that the drop shipper is getting the job done. Copies of the shipping documents or tracking numbers may be all you need for accountability. Make sure you get something. You probably don't have to check every shipment, but at least spot check the shipments to make sure your buyers are getting their items as quickly as possible.

Back Orders

What happens when your drop shipper runs out of stock for the product you're selling? You're in trouble. You can immediately take the product out of your auctions, but there may be at least one sold, or perhaps more, for which there will be no timely delivery. This is a great way to get negative feedback.

You need to immediately handle the situation to pacify the buyer. Your reputation is at stake in a business environment where customer service isn't everything, it's the only thing. Yes, drop shipping has its risks.

Preventives

What can you do to prevent trouble from back orders? Here are a few practices that will work to keep you out of trouble:

- State the possibility of a back order in your auction listing.
- Auction only items of which the drop shipper has a large quantity in stock.
- Closely monitor the quantities remaining in the drop shipper's

stock (via the drop shipper's website or other means).

- Run shorter auctions so there's less chance a product will become back ordered during an auction.

- Cancel the auction if the drop shipper's quantity in stock reaches zero.

- Keep one of the products in perpetual inventory on your premises so that in the event of a back order, you can ship the product yourself.

When the Back Order Occurs

What do you do now? There are a few inexpensive strategies, and if you don't mind spending money, there are even more options:

- Contact your buyer immediately.

- Offer to refund your buyer's money.

- Try to find the item from another supplier.

- Send your buyer a free gift for waiting.

- Leave positive feedback first.

The back order is not necessarily your fault. But that's irrelevant to the customer. Don't blame. In general, use the back order as an opportunity to show off your supurb customer service.

High Wholesale Prices

Wholesale prices for products drop shipped tend to be high. You buy in the lowest possible quantity (one at a time). Volume purchasing dictates wholesale prices. Don't be surprised if you find some drop shipping product prices close to full retail prices. You need to be extraordinarily careful in accessing the potential profitability of selling a product via drop shipping. This is particularly important in industries where the normal retail margins are thin. However, the inexpensive test marketing facilitated by drop shipping reduces your risk of catastrophic losses.

You may be able to take advantage of volume purchasing by using a drop shipping service (see Chapter 13). Some of these services arrange to purchase inventory from suppliers in volume and pass the savings along to their customers (eBay and ecommerce retailers just like you).

Drop Shipping Costs

Drop shipping is not a new idea. Certain suppliers have pushed this idea for decades in an attempt to recruit people into the home mail-order business. The drop shipping suppliers have extended their recruiting efforts to people who want to have an online business. Some of the drop shipping suppliers are legitimate sources of high-quality, profitable products. Others are close to fraud in that their inventory is low quality and the cost of their products is high. It is up to you to decide which ones are reputable.

This is where you have to do some comparative shopping among suppliers. First, you find suppliers of a particular product that do not drop ship. You ask for quotes and get a range of prices. For instance, suppose you asked three wholesalers for wholesale quotes on a single camcorder that you will sell on eBay for about $415:

Wholesaler 1:	$243.15
Wholesaler 2:	$248.23
Wholesaler 3:	$241.76

The range is approximately $241 to $249. Next you look at three drop shipping quotes for the same camcorder:

Drop shipper 1:	$257.85
Drop shipper 2:	$289.62
Drop shipper 3:	$266.91

The range is approximately $257 to $290. You make a rough calculation that your own cost of fulfillment for this product will be about $11. What should you do?

Cost of Fulfillment

If you already run a fulfillment operation, you always need to know what your cost of fulfillment per product is for your inventory. If you don't, you need to start calculating it routinely. If you haven't started your business yet, you need to estimate what your cost of fulfillment per product will be.

There are several possibilities. Let's say you go with the lowest prices. The difference is $16.09 ($257.85 − $241.76 = $16.09). If you already have a fulfillment operation, you can save $5.09 ($16.09 − $11 = $5.09) by doing the shipping and handling yourself. That's a significant amount, and you will probably integrate the camcorder sales into your fulfillment operation. If you don't have your own fulfillment operation, the $5.09 savings by itself probably isn't going to entice you into setting up a fulfillment operation. Therefore, drop shipping seems attractive.

An Even Lower Price

Note that buying in bulk from the supplier would surely result in an even lower price per camcorder than buying one at a time. Typically, the minimum quantity would be a carton, which might have from 6 to 24 camcorders in it.

Saturated Markets

It is not unusual to find certain product markets saturated with sales, particularly markets for commodity products such as electronics. In any case, it's very tough to compete in such markets. Price wars make the retail margins razor thin. And it's impossible to compete in such markets using drop shipping. The higher wholesale prices associated with drop shipping make winning price wars improbable.

Realistically, drop shipping is for niche markets. But then most profitable eBay selling is in niche markets.

Lost Opportunities

If you acquire all your inventory through drop shippers, you give up the opportunity to lower your cost of inventory with volume discounts and closeout purchases. In other words, you always buy at the single-product wholesale price, which is the highest wholesale price.

In fact, your competitors may be able to sell the same product at a lower price on eBay than you can acquire it via drop shippers. This is not always the case, of course, but it's something to watch out for and avoid.

Product Cycle

Profitable drop shipping sales are primarily limited to the growth and maturity stages of the product cycle. Drop shipping generally will not work as well for the introduction and decline stages of the product cycle. Read more about the product cycle in Chapter 1.

Combination Sales

In this chapter we show the difference between doing your own fulfillment and using drop shipping. In reality, you can do both. Why not? If drop shipping provides the most profit for a particular product, use it. If doing your own fulfillment provides the most profit for a product, do it. Stay flexible. As we say numerous times, there is no one-size-fits-all scheme for profitable sales on eBay.

Fraud

There are many fraudulent drop shippers just waiting to take your money without delivering the goods. Read more on this in Chapter 24.

Finding Suppliers

It's not difficult to find drop shipping suppliers. There are plenty of sources that are highly visible. It's your job to choose the ones that can help make your eBay retail business profitable.

Just Ask

If you want drop shipping, ask all the suppliers you talk with whether they provide it. Few suppliers do. Yet more and more suppliers today are starting to provide drop shipping. It's an expanding service, not a shrinking one. You may be surprised to learn who provides it. It doesn't hurt to ask.

Drop Shipping Services

There are a number of services that match up retailers with drop shippers. See Chapter 13 for more about this source. Sometimes they are called drop shipping agents. They can save you a lot of work in attempting to find inventory.

Advertising

Many drop shipping businesses have been around for a long time. You can find them in advertisements in business magazines, particularly magazines catering to small businesses. You can find them at trade shows. They are not invisible.

Customer Service

You can't avoid customer service just because you have hired (in effect) a drop shipper to do your fulfillment. Your customers will still hold you responsible. You need to fold the drop shipping service into your overall customer service.

For instance, it's convenient to send a customer a tracking number for the shipment. That way he or she knows the item has been shipped, and you won't be bothered by inquiries as to when the item will be delivered. Consequently, it's nice—perhaps essential—if a drop shipper sends the tracking number to your customer for you. Indeed, it has become easier and less expensive to do this in the last few years (due to advances in digital technology), and it is quickly becoming a standard.

In other words, when it comes to fulfillment, if your drop shipper doesn't do it for you, you will have to do it yourself.

Summary

Drop shipping is a great way to acquire inventory, but it's not perfect. You relieve yourself of the chores of carrying inventory and operating a fulfillment center. When you buy your inventory from a drop shipping supplier, however, you need to be vigilant about customer service, which is out of your control. Then, too, there are back orders, which may get you in hot water with your customers. But all things considered, it's an alternative you should explore.

8

Consignment

Your object is to make a profit on selling inventory. Normally, you buy the inventory at wholesale and sell it at retail to realize a profit margin that keeps your business viable. But you own the inventory, and if it doesn't sell, you're stuck with it. Or perhaps you can sell it if you cut your margin.

Is consignment selling any different? No. You're still selling inventory. It's the risk that's different. If you don't sell it, you're not stuck with it; it belongs to someone else. And if you have to reduce the price to sell it, your profit is reduced only a nominal amount for a percentage fee and nothing for a flat fee. What a deal!

But there's got to be be a disadvantage, and there is. With consignment selling, you can't just pick up the telephone and order more inventory from a wholesaler. You have to find the inventory.

Consignment Sales

Consignment sales happen when someone wants you to sell their product or products on eBay for them. In this case, you acquire inventory but do not have to pay for it. Your revenue is fixed either by a percentage of the sale price or a specific fee. Usually a consignment sales operations handles one product at a time, or a set of products at one time. There is no ongoing acquisition of identical inventory from the same source.

You can find consignment products two ways. You can set up shop and have consignment customers walk in the door with their products to deposit with you for your subsequent sales on eBay. This, of course, requires a physical location, a store in your community.

The other way is for you to go out and find consignment customers. If you find the sales this way, you do not necessarily have to have a storefront location. But you do have to go around from place to place to drum up business.

So there you are. Either your customers do the walking and create walk-in traffic for you, or you do the walking and go out and find customers. Where can you find customers?

Mandated Auctions

There are many situations in which the law requires that goods be disposed of by auction. This may be a requirement for government surplus, abandoned goods, goods confiscated from criminals, and the like. You may be able to travel around to governmental entities, lawyers, landlords, and law enforcement officials to find inventory that you can sell on eBay. This may work even if the products in question are not mandated to be auctioned. The fact is that eBay is a great marketplace to sell such goods.

If you seek such consignment inventory, do you have to be a licensed auctioneer? That's a question that's difficult to answer. There are 50 different sets of laws in 50 different states that govern this kind of activity. You will have to determine within your own state whether you will need to be a licensed auctioneer or not.

If Not Mandated

If an auction is not mandated for a particular class of goods, you should be able to sell such goods on consignment on eBay without being a licensed auctioneer.

Non-Profit Organizations

One way for non-profit organizations that are charities to raise money is to auction off donated goods. You are probably familiar with a charitable organization in your community that holds silent auctions periodically to raise revenue. People donate products to the charity, and the charity in turn auctions off the products to raise funds. These products are typically auctioned off at a time and place (usually an event) designated by the charity. There's no reason they couldn't be auctioned off on eBay. In fact, eBay has proven a fruitful place to raise revenue for charities. This is a potential source of inventory for you that is essentially a source of consignment inventory.

Garage Sales

Garage sales often sell only a small percentage of those items put up for sale on the day and place of the garage sale. By visiting garage sales you may be able to pick up consignment customers that have more than one product for you to sell on eBay.

Beat the Bushes

You can see where we're going with this. If you're not going to have a walk-in consignment store, you have to get out in the community and beat the bushes for consignment items to sell from such sources as probate lawyers (estates); bankruptcy lawyers (bankrupt estates); and businesses, agricultural businesses, and governments (equipment and excess supplies). And don't overlook artists and craftspeople.

We have given you a few examples here, but there are many more. Let your imagination be your guide. Naturally, you will gravitate to clients who give you repeat business such as businesses, organizations and government agencies.

Consignment Fees

Your fee for a consignment sale can be a flat fee or a commission (percentage). Fees vary widely. You will need to inquire locally to see what the competition is charging and use that information to establish a fee schedule for your services. In addition, you will need to charge your sellers for any expenses such as eBay fees, packaging, and shipping.

One of the nice features of consignment sales is that you don't have to worry about margins. You get your fee regardless of the economics of the transaction. In effect, you set your own margin.

Good Start

Consignment sales on eBay (without a store) are a financially painless way to get off to a good start in your eBay retailing career. With the experience you gain, you can bide your time as you search for the perfect niche and the requisite suppliers, and then you can jump out of consignment into a normal retailing operation. But who knows? You may find consignment sales to be just the ticket for you.

Don't Have to Choose

You don't have to choose between consignment sales and normal retail sales. Many eBay retailers do both.

Consignment Stores

Consignment stores are nothing new. What's new is that consignment stores can now sell products on eBay as well as selling them out of the store.

What's also new is consignment stores that make no attempt to sell products out of their store. They operate the store simply to get walk-in customers for consignment sales that the store makes on eBay.

Do these stores work? They can. In some places they work and in other places they don't. The only benefit they provide compared to a consignment business without a store is that they provide a place for walk-in customers. If a consignment store is well-located for walk-in traffic, it might be successful. If not, it can be a risky way to start a consignment business.

Consignment Store Franchises

Are consignment store franchises worthwhile? That depends on what you need. There is no consignment store franchise today that has an established brand. They are all too new. Therefore, it may be a long time before their branding is a benefit to your consignment store operation. The one thing they can do for you is provide you with consignment software and consignment systems for handling products and eBay auctions that you might otherwise have to cobble together yourself.

If you are clever with computers and understand how to set up systems for handling products efficiently, you probably don't need a franchise.

If you are digitally inept and have never worked in a situation where you have to handle products, package them, and ship them, a franchise offering may be valuable to you.

Auction Management Software

Today many auction management services include a consignment sales component or offer one at an additional cost.

A typical franchise fee is about $15,000. However, many franchises will require you to spend the money to set up what they consider to be proper systems. Thus, the typical setup for an eBay consignment store franchise will cost you somewhere between $70,000 and $100,000. That may seem like a large amount, but in order to evaluate such a fee objectively, you will have to compare it to what it will cost you to set up a consignment store and a consignment operation without a consignment franchise. Depending on how you do it, it could cost less, or it could cost more. Also, keep in mind that the franchise fee doesn't cover rent and other ongoing overhead for your consignment store.

There are a few consignment franchises that have a very low cost, usually under $1,000. These are not consignment store franchises. They're just consignment franchises intended for people without consignment stores. Because of their low cost, they might be a good deal for you for two reasons:

- They will provide you with useful information on how to start and operate your consignment business without a consignment store.

- Through their branding, they may give you additional credibility that you would not otherwise have. This may be true even if the brand today has little brand recognition among general consumers.

All things considered, it is much too early to tell whether consignment sale franchises are worthwhile either for consignment stores or just for eBay consignment businesses without stores. Therefore, if you decide to purchase a franchise, start a consignment business, and use this method of acquiring inventory, you are something of a pioneer today.

Here is a list of current franchisors for eBay consignment sales storefronts:

AuctionDrop, *http://auctiondrop.com* (This is now part of UPS Stores for UPS Store franchisees that want to use it.)

iSoldIt, *http://i-soldit.com*

QuikDrop, *http://quikdrop.com*

SnappyAuctions, *http://snappyauctions.com*

United Auction Brokers, *http://www.unitedauctionbrokers.com* (This is not a storefront but rather a pick-up-and-sell eBay consignment service. It is an inexpensive franchise with low overhead.)

Note that consignment sales on eBay make a sensible part-time business for business-services locations such as UPS Stores, Kinko's (now owned by FedEx), and PostNet.

Figure 8.1 SnappyAuctions website.

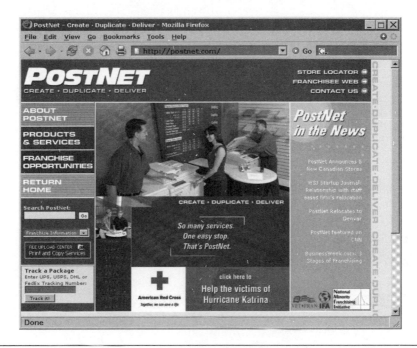

Figure 8.2 PostNet website. ©2005 PostNet International Franchise Corporation. All rights reserved.

Read more about consignment sales in *eBay the Smart Way*, Second Edition, or *How to Start and Run an eBay Consignment Business* (Skip McGrath, McGraw-Hill Osborne Media, 2006).

Summary

You may not think about consignment sales as an inventory acquisition scheme. But it provides free inventory until you sell it. You don't pay for the inventory until after you sell it, when you pass the sales price on to your seller-customer, less your consignment fee. And you can set your own margin, that is, your consignment fee.

This is an inventory acquisition scheme that requires constant activity (or a store) to generate items to sell. But you don't have to find a niche and you risk only your time but not much of your money (assuming you don't have a store). It has proven a popular and profitable way to join the eBay retailing profession.

III

Sources

9

Trade Markets

Trade markets are places where suppliers and retailers come together to look over, evaluate, negotiate, and contract for products to be acquired by retailers for subsequent retail sales. This is one of the best ways to find products—particularly new products—to sell on eBay or otherwise sell online. It's often a lot of trouble and sometimes expensive to attend trade shows, particularly when they're out of town. Yet it's one of the best ways you can spend your time, particularly when you're in a start-up situation or when you're otherwise looking for new products to supplement existing product lines. Trade shows usually take place in convention centers, large hotels, and trade marts.

Trade Shows

Trade shows make a great beginning for your quest to find products you can sell profitably on eBay. The term "trade shows" as used in this book means wholesale trade shows. Trade shows for consumers are referred to as "consumer shows."

Wholesale trade shows are great places to search for eBay inventory for many reasons:

- Most are closed to the public.

- Most are open to those with a sales tax license.

- They are a place for new products to be unveiled.

- They are a place to get detailed information on products and hands-on assessments of products.

- They are a place to get information on an industry, or in some cases, multiple industries.

- They include small manufacturers and producers that might be difficult to find otherwise.

- Large trade shows, particularly regional and national trade shows, have a large variety of products.

- They are places to get good deals such as product introductions or closeouts.

- They are places to negotiate good deals.

- You can take advantage of special pricing (e.g., show specials) only offered at the show.

- They are places to make valuable contacts.

- They are places to learn.

Food Show

In one day at one regional food trade show in 1994 that Joe attended with his food entrepreneur clients, they were able to get about two dozen unique gourmet food products from different companies. Joe put these in an online catalog for his clients that became the first gourmet food store on the Web. Some of the products were new at the time and have proven so successful since that they eventually migrated into the supermarkets.

Local

Local trade shows are usually intended for consumers as well as retailers. They are usually local in scope. Regional and national manufacturers and wholesalers usually don't attend, although there will always be a few that do. Usually at local shows, the emphasis is on the consumer. Nonetheless, it may be a good opportunity for you to find manufacturers and wholesalers that will do business with you. It may also be an opportunity to find new products.

The nice thing about local trade shows is that they're convenient. You can take a day or a half-day off work, and after a short drive each way the time you spend will be cost-effective. Yet local trade shows are rarely as productive as regional or national trade shows.

Regional

Regional trade shows are seldom intended for consumers as well as retailers. They are usually strictly for retailers and you will have to prove that you are a retailer to gain admittance. You usually do this by showing your sales tax license. You will often find suppliers at regional trade shows that do not go to the national trade shows. They are too small and their budgets don't allow for the higher expense of marketing their wares at national trade shows. On the other hand, some national manufacturers and wholesalers will not be present at regional trade shows. They put their money into making a big splash at the national trade show but don't have the budget to also market their products at 20 or 30 different regional trade shows.

If a regional trade show is held in your city, it's just like a local trade show, only with greater benefits for you. However, if it's held in a nearby city, it will likely be almost as expensive as going to a national trade show in a distant city. With today's air fares and hotel costs, flying to a city 2,500 miles away is often no more expensive than going to a city that's 500 miles away. It will take you one day's travel time each way, plus a few days at the trade show itself. Thus, you are talking about at least a several-day commitment.

On the other hand, if you can drive or fly to a regional trade show in half a day, you will save a day and thus reduce the time commitment to attending.

National

National trade shows are usually the best events for you to attend to find the benefits listed above. National trade shows can be very productive not only when you're just getting started, but also when you're seeking new inventory for an existing product line that you sell. Even small companies attempt to exhibit at national trade shows. They can cover the entire United States that way instead of just covering one region, for a cost that is higher than attending a regional trade show but substantially lower than attending multiple regional trade shows. Indeed, it is usually the new companies and the small companies that have the innovative new products that might be particularly appropriate for your eBay retail operation.

Of course, the big manufacturers and wholesalers are always at the national trade shows because that is a cost-effective way for them to market their products.

Determining the Type of Show

How do you tell the difference between a regional and national trade show? Well, it might be in the name of the show or description of the show. But sometimes it's hard to tell. Ask if you can't find out any other way. You may regret going to a show you thought was national, which turned out to be a three-state show.

How to Work a Trade Show

In the old days, having a corporation and other legal signs of business identity might have given you the credibility you needed to get wholesalers to take you seriously. That's been so overdone that we don't think it works well any longer. What you need is a good story and the capability to conduct yourself in a business-like manner.

Preregister

Always preregister for trade shows. You usually get a price break and don't have to stand in line to register. More important, by registering in advance, you may get invited to some lavish parties (great for networking) thrown by large companies and even small ones.

What You Take

Go to a trade show with what you need to identify yourself as a retailer. You can inquire ahead of time what's required. For many shows, a sales tax license is the ticket of admission. Other trade shows may require a business license or a tax ID number. And always take dozens and dozens of business cards.

Wholesalers

Wholesalers may ask for the same things as the show sponsor, so be ready to provide such information as the standard means of doing business everywhere. Chapter 5 provides a complete list.

If you expect to get credit from wholesalers, you may need copies of your financial statements and other credit documents. Such documents might come in handy, as you can often do business right at the show.

It's always handy to have a small calculator. And we don't have to tell you how handy a cell phone can be when you're doing business.

Finally, you need to bring your checkbook. You may be able to make a favorable purchase on the spot. Before purchasing anything, however, see the whole show first.

Get to the show early and ready to go the first morning. Competition is often fierce. You can't know your best purchase until you've seen all the merchandise. Another reason to see the whole show early is to be one of the first retailers to take advantage of show specials and new products of limited distribution.

Laptop

You might want to take your laptop along (with wireless network capability) to check eBay auctions when you need to. If you find a surplus sale on 10 dozen silk ties, you need to check out eBay to determine what the market is for silk ties before you make such a purchase.

Telling Your Story

Your story needs to be well thought out ahead of time—and it should be honest. If you are just starting your eBay business, don't hide it. Everyone will eventually figure it out anyway. Let people know. Tell people about the serious steps you have taken to get your eBay business off the ground. Mention what distinguishes you from an eBay hobbyist. Everyone loves a good story. Make yours personal, honest, interesting, and short. You will get some unexpected help from folks.

Make Your Status Work for You

Use your start-up status as a retailer to talk suppliers into providing you with free samples, to buy small quantities of products that are otherwise only available in large quantities, or to get other concessions. Negotiation is the name of this game.

Business-Like Presence

Dress in appropriate business clothes. In some parts of the country that might mean a suit or dress. In most parts of the country casual business clothes are acceptable for trade shows. Wear comfortable shoes. If you're doing your job well, you'll walk a lot of miles on the exhibition floor. Take a lot of business cards along to hand out. All industries float on business cards. Be confident. Your confidence attracts people's attention.

Also present a professional appearence on paper (e.g., custom business cards, letterhead, purchase orders, etc.) and in person (e.g., briefcase, calculator, digital camera, etc.). One of those business organizers on wheels (looks like a small suitcase or large briefcase) is appropriate to tow around. Don't forget, you'll be taking home a lot of product literature and even samples.

Be friendly but stick to the point. Sure, small talk is great, but turn the conversation to the business at hand, which is selling products at retail. That's what the wholesalers are there for, and that's what you're there for. Visit every booth and listen carefully. You can never learn too much, and you can't learn when you're doing the talking. Note on the back of each business card you collect something to remind you of the individual. Even take notes on important conversations, special offerings, meaningful observations, and ideas that pop into your head. It doesn't hurt to take a pocket digital camera either, although generally there is plenty of product literature with nice product photographs.

Sound like fun? It can be. But it's work too. If you're a successful eBay retailer, it's part of what you do.

Who's in Charge?

Most of the time, you're in charge. Most suppliers want you as a customer. Nonetheless, some are fussy about to whom they sell. Such suppliers often have good reason to be fussy. They have great products in high demand, and they want to protect their successful retailer customers by not diluting the market too much. If you're interested in their products, you're going to have to talk them into taking you on as a retailer. Your best technique here is to ask probing questions, then listen. Listen a lot. You can often figure out a way to become one of their retailers (dealers) even if it requires a long-term strategy.

Retail Location

Some suppliers will require you to have a physical retail location. Joe knows one eBay business that does 90 percent of its sales on eBay and 10 percent out of its retail store. But without the retail store, it can't buy the brand-name inventory.

Hard to Beat

Let us state without reservation that regional and national trade shows are excellent places to find good products to buy at wholesale and sell on eBay, particularly new and innovative products. Go for it!

Education

Many trade shows have seminars and even courses where you can learn a lot about an industry and its products. Some shows even have comprehensive educational schedules. Don't go to a trade show without spending some time learning and keeping up to date. Often the information presented is not available elsewhere.

Finding Trade Shows

Some trade show websites where you can find trade show schedules follow:

ASD/AMD, *http://www.merchandisegroup.com* (exhibitor at eBay Live conference – see Figure 9.1)

Computer Digital Expo Las Vegas, *http://www.internettradeshow list.com*

EventsEye, *http://www.eventseye.com*

Global Sources Trade Show Center, *http://tradeshow.global sources.com/TRADESHW/TRDSHFRM.HTM?referrer=adwords*

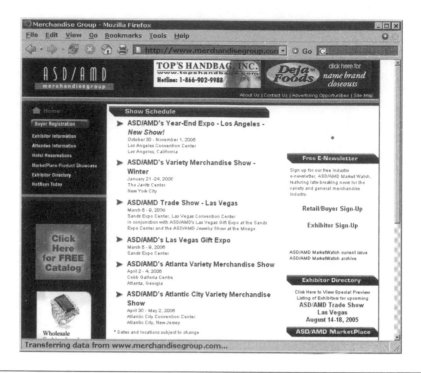

Figure 9.1 ASD/AMD website. ©2005 VNU eMedia Inc. All rights reserved.

Greatrep, *http://greatrep.com*

NAMM, *http://www.namm.com/tradeshow*

Tradeshowbiz.com, *http://www.tradeshowbiz.com*

Trade Show Plaza, *http://www.tradeshowplaza.com*

Tradeshow Week, *http://www.tradeshowweek.com*

TSNN.com, *http://www.tsnn.com*

Yahoo directory, *http://dir.yahoo.com/Business_and_Economy/ Business_to_Business/Conventions_and_Trade_Shows*

And finally, you can purchase a printed trade show directory featuring over 10,000 trade shows in over 100 countries:

- International Tradeshow Directory, *http://www.iaem.org/content/ITD.pdf*
- ExpoWorld Tradeshows Worldwide Directory, *http://www.expo-world.com/signup.asp?sid=0*

Online Directory (Schedule)

There's nothing better than an online directory of trade shows that's a schedule too and is always current. Here are two examples from the list above.

Tradeshow Week

Tradeshow Week is a publication that is aimed at personnel and companies that put on trade shows. As such, you won't have much interest in subscribing to Tradeshow Week or the information that Tradeshow Week publishes. Nonetheless, at the Tradeshow Week website (*http://www.tradeshowweek.com*) you can find a directory (schedule) of trade shows. The directory is organized alphabetically and also by product type. The website provides a database mechanism wherein you can search for the type of trade shows that you need to attend and find out when and where they will be held. This database covers the entire world, not just the United States. So Joe would say to you that the one most important thing you can do is find the trade show for the products you intend to sell and attend that trade show wherever it might be.

A Tradeshow Week directory search for just Food & Beverage shows in the United States (Fall 2005) yielded the following (strictly an example):

All Asia Food Expo (Los Angeles)

All Asia Food Expo (New York)

Americas Food & Beverage Show (Miami)

Southeast Michigan Holiday Beverage Show (Livonia)

Atlantic City Gourmet Food & Cooking Festival

Coffee Fest Seattle

Expo Comida Latina (Los Angeles)

National Automatic Merchandising Association (Atlanta)

North American Specialty Beverage Retailers Expo (Denver)

National Beer Wholesalers Association Expo (Las Vegas)

National Gourmet Food Show (Dallas)

National Products Expo East (Washington)

Philadelphia National Candy, Gift & Gourmet Show

Private Label Trade Show (Chicago)

SOHO Expo (Orlando)

South Carolina Foodservice Expo (Myrtle Beach)

National Association of Convenience Stores Show (New Orleans)

Western Food Industry Expo (Las Vegas)

Wine Expo of the Americas (Miami Beach)

The above search example shows that you can easily find trade shows relevant to your products.

EventsEye

EventsEye (*http://www.eventseye.com*) is another trade show directory that includes dates and covers the entire world. Below are the results of a search on international shows for the month of October 2005 (strictly an example):

Kabul International Trade Fair (Afghanistan)

International Engineering Fair (Czech Republic)

Technical International Bucharest Fair (Romania)

Zaragoza General Trade Fair (Spain)

Ramadan Commercial Days (Casablanca, Morocco)

International Versatile Expo (Bishkek, Kyrgyzstan)

Mumbai International Trade Fair (India)

Public Entertainment & Direct Selling Expo (Abu Dhabi, UAE)

Canton Fair at the China Foreign Trade Centre (see Figure 9.2)

Figure 9.2 Canton Fair in China. ©2005 China Foreign Trade Centre. All rights reserved.

International Fair of Monaco

Fair of Jura (Lons-le-Saunier, France)

Luxembourg International Trade Fair

Kenya International Trade Expo (Nairobi)

Agricultural Commercial & Industrial Fair (Girona, Spain)

Commercial Fair (Basel, Switzerland)

Havana International Fair (Cuba)

Again, the above search example shows that you can find general and even international trade shows quite easily.

International

You often have to travel to international trade shows because they are held in other countries such as Japan and Germany. It's smart, however, to be aware of international trade shows being held in the United States. The United States gets its share of international trade shows just like other countries do. An international trade show can be your cost-effective entrée into the world of import/export.

In fact, some international trade shows are often held in the United States for the specific purpose of manufacturers and wholesalers finding retailers to market their products in the United States. There is more on international trade in Chapter 25.

Local Exhibit Halls

To find local trade shows you need not do more than check the schedule of your local exhibit places. The convention center or other exhibit places will usually publish a calendar at least a year in advance, and often earlier than that, which shows each event that will take place at the exhibit place during the coming year. Some of those events will be trade shows. If it's a trade show that fits products that you are considering, it gives you a prime opportunity to get some firsthand information on the products and meet some suppliers.

It also will pay off to check the convention center schedules in other cities. Cities such as New York, Orlando, Miami, Las Vegas, Los Angeles, San Francisco, and others are popular places for conferences and trade shows. Many put their schedules on the Web.

Trade Marts

A trade mart is like a trade show but in a permanent location where it operates year round. Trade marts have various names such as merchandise mart, fashion mart, design center, gift mart, and others.

If you live in a sizeable city, you may have a trade mart in your city. You can go to the trade mart and find that each manufacturer and wholesaler has rented a small, or sometimes large, space in the trade mart to exhibit its products. This can make finding products very easy for you. Perhaps the most well known example of a trade mart is the Merchandise Mart in Chicago, which is a huge building housing hundreds and hundreds of manufacturers and wholesalers. It has been owned by the Kennedy family for many years.

If you don't have a trade mart in your city, you may live near a larger city that does have a trade mart. It is certainly worth your time and effort to make a visit to that trade mart, even though you will have to travel to do so. Once you have made that visit to the trade mart, you will become well aware of whether it's worth a return visit. It's always there whenever you want to travel.

A partial list of permanent trade mart buildings in the US follows:

225 Fifth Avenue, *http://www.225-fifth.com* (New York – home furnishings)

AmericasMart, *http://www.americasmart.com* (Atlanta – general merchandise – see Figure 9.3)

California Market Center, *http://www.californiamarketcenter.com* (Los Angeles – fashion, gifts, and home decor)

Charlotte Merchandise Mart, *http://www.charlottemerchmart.com* (general merchandise)

Figure 9.3 AmericasMart. ©2003 Americasmart.com. All rights reserved.

Chicago Merchandise Mart, *http://www.mmart.com* (clothing, gifts, and home accessories)

Columbus Marketplace, *http://www.columbusgiftmart.com* (gifts, garden, and home accessories)

Dallas Market Center, *http://www.dallasmarketcenter.com* (general merchandise)

Denver Merchandise Mart, *http://www.denvermart.com* (gifts, clothing, and interior design)

International Home Furnishings Center, *http://www.ihfc.com* (High Point, North Carolina – home furnishings)

Kansas City Gift Mart, *http://www.kcgiftmart.com* (gifts, gourmet food and implements, and home accessories – see Figure 9.4)

Kitchen Bath Building Design Center, *http://www.kitchenbath-center.com* (Chicago, Washington, and New York – kitchen and bath furnishings and decor)

Miami Merchandise Mart, *http://miamimart.net* (clothing, home accessories, and electronics)

LA Mart, *http://www.mmart.com/lamart* (Los Angeles – designer home furnishings and decor)

Michigan Gift Mart, *http://www.michigangiftmart.com* (Northville – gifts)

Minneapolis Gift Mart, *http://www.mplsgiftmart.com* (gifts)

New Mart, *http://www.newmart.net* (Los Angeles – designer clothes)

New York Merchandise Mart, *http://www.41madison.com* (home accessories)

Northeast Market Center, *http://thegiftcenter.com* (near Boston – gifts)

Pacific Design Center, *http://www.pacificdesigncenter.com* (West Hollywood, California – home decor and accessories)

Ronald Reagan Building and International Trade Center, *http:// www.itcdc.com* (Washington)

San Francisco Gift Center, *http://gcjm.com* (fashion and jewelry)

Seattle Gift Center, *http://seattlegiftcenter.com* (gifts)

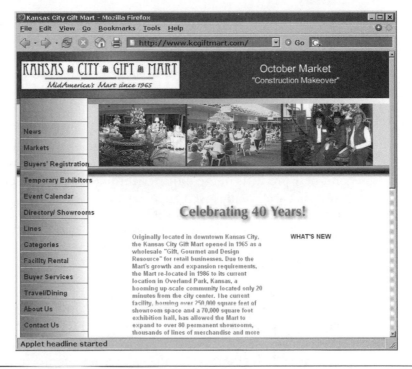

Figure 9.4 Kansas City Gift Mart. ©2004 Rossini.com. All rights reserved.

Consumer Shows

Consumer shows can also be a good place to pursue product ideas. Although the shows are intended for consumers, you can sometimes find personnel attending the show as part of a supplier's exhibit that are the ones that you would normally talk with to acquire inventory. And if such personnel are not in the supplier's exhibit, the people who are there may be able to refer you to the proper people.

In any event, consumer shows often give you a firsthand view of existing products and new products, enabling you to evaluate such products firsthand. Consequently, you should be aware of the consumer shows that will come to your city and put them on your schedule for attendance. In fact, it may be worth your while to attend consumer shows in other nearby cities.

Lists

None of the lists in this chapter (or book) are comprehensive. Nor will the lists be current by the time you read the book. Fortunately, you can use Google or another search engine to augment the lists included or to create your own custom lists. This is what you do as a retailer to find places where you can acquire inventory.

Summary

Joe believes that trade shows are one terrific place to find inventory. On top of that, they're a great place to learn about new developments and new products in the industry through the seminars and presentations that are usually given ancillary to a trade show. In addition, trade shows give you a great opportunity to cut deals immediately, or at least make immediate contact with the people with whom you can cut a deal for inventory within a few weeks after the show. It doesn't get any better than this.

On the other hand, Jeremy likes the drop shipping business, which you can learn about in Chapter 7. You might think that using a drop shipping service like Jeremy's Doba would mean that you never have to attend a trade show. Not so. Jeremy encourages all his retail customers to attend trade shows. He doesn't see it as competition but rather as an opportunity for his customers to learn a lot and become more comfortable with products that they will sell.

10

Trade Organizations

Trade or industrial organizations usually cover an industry of related products. Although such organizations are started and operated by people who are working in the industry, they typically receive financial and other support from companies in the industry. They provide you with an excellent opportunity to network and make excellent contacts within the industry, contacts that will lead you directly or indirectly to the kind of products you seek to sell. And they are a great means of learning about products and marketing. In addition, they can provide you with the education and credibility to achieve greater success sooner.

National Trade Organizations

National trade organizations abound. Go to your library to the reference section to research what organizations might fit your retail business (see example in Figure 10.1).

Education

National trade organizations provide you with an excellent opportunity to learn more about the industry you are in, the products, the way people use the products, and new developments within the industry.

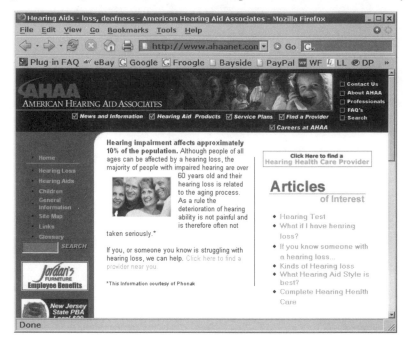

Figure 10.1 American Hearing Aid Associates website. ©2002 American Hearing Aid Associates. All rights reserved.

This can be a valuable resource for you and your business. To be a first-rate and profitable retailer, you should be an expert in the products you sell and aware of what's going on in the industry.

National Conference

Most major trade organizations hold a national conference each year at which you can attend seminars, make contacts, and also become acquainted with particular vendors that serve the industry. The national conference put on by a trade organization is one of the major benefits to being in a trade organization, and you should plan on attending as often as possible.

Networking

Your prime reason for being in a trade organization is to network with others in the organization. Presumably the others in the organization are suppliers with whom you can potentially do business. In addition, you are likely to meet fellow retailers from whom you can learn.

Because via eBay you are selling to a national audience, you will want to have access to national manufacturers and wholesalers. Being in a trade organization is an easy way to get in touch with the people who represent such companies. Talk to other people who are in the industry and ask them about the trade organizations they belong to and the annual meetings they have attended. We believe they will agree that participating in such annual conferences is a great way to network as well as learn.

Trade Show

Some trade organizations actually sponsor major trade shows, and such trade shows act as the annual national conferences for the organizations as well. If this is true for your industry organization, you can kill two birds with one stone. You will get all the benefits of a trade organization conference as well as all the benefits of a national trade show.

Statistics

National trade organizations often provide industry statistics and other information that can prove useful to your market analyses. Normally, some of the information is public, some for members only.

Focus

Different trade organizations focus on different communities within an industry. A few trade organizations encompass all communities within the industry.

Manufacturers

If the trade organization you want to join caters only to manufacturers, you may not be eligible for admission and may not be eligible to attend the annual national conference. However, when such organizations are exclusive, they sometimes admit people who are not manufacturers as second-class members with limited participation privileges. Thus, you still may be able to join.

Wholesalers

Again, some national trade organizations may be just for wholesalers. Or, they may be just for manufacturers and wholesalers. Don't let that deter you from seeking membership. There may be a second-class membership that will enable you to become a participant.

Retailers

If the organization is strictly for retailers, you will want to investigate the possibilities for networking with manufacturers and wholesalers.

Networking

Certainly there are a lot of benefits of belonging to a purely retail trade organization, and we encourage you to join any that are available to you. Nonetheless, since the objective in this book is to make contacts that will lead you to products, new products, and adequate inventory for your eBay business, participation in a retail trade organization may not provide what you need.

If the retail trade organization holds an annual conference or sponsors a trade show where you can meet suppliers, that is the benefit you are looking for, which will make such a retail trade organization more valuable to you.

Exchanges

There is another aspect of associating with other retailers around the country that leads to acquiring inventory. You can make inventory exchanges.

This is a misnomer. Although inventory transfers are often done between retailers through exchange networks or organizations, the transfer is normally just a sale and purchase. In other words, such an association may provide you with the opportunity to buy excess inventory from another retailer or sell your excess inventory to another retailer.

Some exchange networks are set up to handle sales systematically and efficiently (e.g., online). Others take an informal approach. But even if you have to call (telephone) around to find inventory, other retailers are a potential source. And the larger the organization, the more potential exists.

Local Chapters

Many national trade organizations have local chapters. If you can find one within a reasonable distance of where you are located, there are benefits to attending the monthly meetings. These are the same benefits you get from a national conference only on a smaller scale.

Local chapters are usually aggressive in sponsoring national education presented locally. And, of course, they provide an opportunity to network.

One problem that many work-at-home eBay retailers have is that it's easy to never leave the office. A monthly chapter meeting gets you out of the house and can be a solid boost to morale while at the same time furthering your retailing career.

Credibility

A lot of people don't understand eBay, and it's likely to be a long time before many people come to fully understand eBay. For instance, if you were to ask a manufacturer or a wholesaler the average net sales of an eBay retailer, they might guess at $4,000 a month, thinking that most eBay retailers were small part-time businesses. The reality is that there are eBay businesses that have gross sales of over $1,000,000 a month with a small number of employees. Those may not be typical eBay retailers, but the range of sales volume for eBay retailers covers an incredibly wide gamut. You want manufacturers and wholesalers, and even other retailers, to take you seriously. That may be difficult to do without explaining your eBay business to everyone you meet.

However, membership in a trade organization gives you instant credibility that you may not otherwise have. Just the fact that you have the professionalism to join a trade organization is a signal to everyone that you're serious and you're successful in the retail business. We recommend that you go so far as to list your membership in a trade organization on your business card.

Don't Overlook eBay

At least one of your trade organizations is eBay. And eBay has an annual conference in June. Not only can you learn a lot there by attending seminars, but you will find a few wholesale suppliers among the exhibitors there too. Missing this annual conference is not a good way to be frugal with your time or money.

Summary

If you can find a trade organization that relates to the products you sell, you may find it beneficial to join. One of the benefits is finding sources of inventory through networking. Others include education, trade shows, contact with other retailers, and credibility. And if you work at home, getting out of the house for a monthly chapter meeting can be the highlight of the week.

11

Manufacturers

A manufacturer is the ultimate source, the root of the supplier-retailer chain. The most profitable relationship for retailers is almost always to buy direct from the manufacturer. Unfortunately, that is seldom possible because most manufacturers require high-volume orders. Still, manufacturers can be helpful. They are usually easy to identify (i.e., from the products they make). They are easy to contact because you can get their contact information from a directory (see Chapter 15). Once contacted, they will be happy to send you to the appropriate wholesaler. That makes finding a place to buy your inventory easy. No secrets here.

Typical Manufacturer

A typical manufacturer manufactures products; that's where it puts its capital and other resources. It sells its products in large quantities to distributors (wholesalers). This process saves the manufacturer from having to run a distribution operation itself.

A distribution operation is a much different business activity from manufacturing. Many manufacturers realize this and stick to manufacturing while letting wholesalers distribute the products in smaller quantities to retailers. This is a relationship that enables each to do what it does best, most efficiently, and most profitably.

Of course, there is no such thing as a "typical" manufacturer. Some have a marketing program that uses manufacturer's reps rather than relying on wholesalers. Some sell into multiple distribution channels. Some even sell directly to retailers (see Figure 11.1). Indeed, a few sell directly to consumers.

There is no reason to avoid contacting any manufacturer for the purpose of acquiring inventory. In fact, if you know what you want, the manufacturer is perhaps the best place to start looking. If it does sell directly to retailers, which is rare, you've found a home. If it doesn't, you can at least get a referral to the proper wholesaler for your geographical area. Indeed, the manufacturer may be the best place to find a wholesaler.

Contact Information

Read Chapter 15 about directories. If you know the manufacturer that you want to contact, there is a directory that will provide you with the contact information.

Many manufacturers are fussy about who they permit to sell their products at retail and how. They have restrictive policies and even dealerships (a particular set of restrictions). They enforce such restrictions through their manufacturer's reps or through their wholesalers.

The most profitable relationship is for you to buy directly from a manufacturer. That should be your goal wherever possible, assuming you can buy inventory in small enough quantities to minimize your risk and stay within the bounds of your financial capabilities. In most cases, however, you will have to buy from a wholesaler. Hey, that's not so bad. You will be able to buy in smaller quantities and take less risk, but the price you pay will be a little higher.

Small Manufacturer

Small manufacturers often have limited marketing budgets and small marketing departments. They are successful because they have established relationships with a number of wholesalers that buy enough

Figure 11.1 Rollings Jewelry, a manufacturer, sells at wholesale online. ©2002 Rollings Jewelry. All rights reserved.

products to keep the manufacturer in business. Often there are untapped channels that would be good places for them to sell their products, but they don't have the marketing horsepower to reach those markets.

Local

If you can find such a small manufacturer in your community, you may be able to walk in and acquire products to sell on eBay. They may welcome you as an opportunity to sell into an untapped market (i.e., the Web). In fact, most small manufacturers are local operations that have only one manufacturing facility. The fact that you are local—and presumably can establish your creditability with your eBay retail experience—will create the potential for a relationship and the opportunity to sell good products that may not be available everywhere. You will need to have a pretty good story to pull this off, but it's worth a try.

National

Local doesn't necessarily mean geographically local any longer. If you're in a trade organization and make contact with a small manufacturer that's also a member of the trade organization, that may usher in an opportunity for you to develop the same kind of relationship with the manufacturer, just as if the manufacturer were in your locale. In this case, the small manufacturer is in your locale, but the locale is not your hometown; it's a national organization.

Special-Order Manufacturers

By special-order manufacturers, we mean manufacturers who sell standard products that they customize for their retail customers in large quantities. This provides you with an opportunity to get mass-produced products that are made especially for you.

Events

A good example is a manufacturer that mass-produces beer mugs. For a certain minimum order, it will put your information on a pewter beer mug. For instance, suppose there's a local marathon that has 2,000 participants and 3,000 spectators. They are all candidates to buy a beer mug that commemorates the annual marathon. You can sell the mugs at a booth at the starting or finish line, in local classified advertising, on Craig's List, and on eBay. When you are selling them locally, you can also indicate to potential buyers that they can go home and order them on eBay.

In fact, there is no reason you cannot do commemorative products for events in other cities. Even national events are good opportunities for marketing these kinds of products.

Joe knows a person who reserved a segment of production time in a manufacturer's schedule to have commemorative pewter mugs made commemorating the World Series. As soon as his team won the American League pennant, he immediately provided the manufacturer with the commemorative information to be etched on the pewter mug. The mugs were manufactured immediately and delivered before the World Series started. His one-time sales project was a very successful one.

Organizations

Providing products that include the name of an organization (e.g., a large corporation or a non-profit organization) may create profitable retail opportunities. The organization has to have enough members to make such an effort profitable. Only a percentage of the organization's members will buy your product. Again, such a sales effort might work for local organizations, but is likely to work better for national organizations with more members. In fact, members of national organizations are more likely to look on eBay to buy such products than are members of organizations that are strictly local.

Licensing

Unfortunately, in most cases, the event or organization that your special products endorse may charge a licensing fee for the information that you put on the custom products. This is particularly true if you use the organization's or the event's name or logo. This is something you will want to investigate before you go to the trouble of arranging your limited manufacturing effort.

If you violate an organization's copyright or trademark, it can quickly get a court order to enjoin your sales. If it doesn't do that before the fact, it can collect damages from you after the fact. Consequently, it's in your own best interest to make sure that you get permission and pay any licensing fees for this kind of sales endeavor.

Other Applications

This idea is not limited to events and organizations. Mass-manufactured products with custom-manufactured attributes are available from many sources, particularly if you can buy in large quantities.

Remanufacturers

Many manufacturers have remanufacturing operations. They have products that are sufficiently expensive and sufficiently easy to repair that they find it profitable to take products returned under warranty and repair them for resale.

In some states, they may have to take the products apart, discard the defective parts, and use the remaining parts in a reassembly process. In other states, they may only have to replace the defective parts. In any event, what matters to you is that you can get name-brand products, straight from the factory in a factory-sealed package, that you can sell at a significant reduction in price compared to the manufacturer's new products.

Third-Parties

Some manufacturers license their remanufacturing to third-parties. Consequently, you make arrangements to sell remanufactured products with the licensed third-party, not the manufacturer.

Typically, established retailers don't want to handle remanufactured products because they compete with the new products that the retailers sell everyday. Consequently, these name-brand manufacturers may be willing to sell remanufactured inventory to you, even if you are not one of their dealers.

You will find this going on all over eBay. Thus, if you can find a product for which no remanufactured products are being sold, it may be an opportunity for you to create some profitable sales. It's just a matter of making contact with the right person at a manufacturer who can arrange to sell you the remanufactured products.

Keep in mind that these products are really not second-class products. They're name-brand products. As name-brand products, they are likely to be high quality. They come straight from the manufacturer, which is some guarantee that they will function as well as new products. And they are priced lower than identical new products. We have purchased many remanufactured products and have been quite happy with them. So our message to you is not to overlook this significant opportunity to acquire inventory.

Summary

Manufacturers are the root source of all inventory. If you can buy direct in quantities you can afford, do so to keep your wholesale costs as low as possible.

Manufacturers are also a great place to start your search for inventory. If you know the product, you can usually determine the manufacturer. If you know the manufacturer, you can get contact information through a directory (see Chapter 15). If the manufacturer doesn't sell direct, it will refer you to the regional distributor for your locale.

In short, manufacturers make great resources for finding inventory, one way or another.

12

Wholesalers

Wholesalers are the source for successful retailers. Sure, you might be able to buy directly from some manufacturers, but you will do most of your inventory business with wholesalers. And where do you find them? There are no secrets about that. You find them by looking for them, and starting with manufacturers is a good way to get going. You can also do something as simple as look them up in the telephone book. But before you take the time to read this chapter, take the time first to read Chapter 5 about supplier-retailer relationships. That will give you the background to deal with them when you do find them.

Typical Wholesalers

A typical wholesaler acts as the distributor for a manufacturer. It warehouses large quantities of manufacturer's goods for subsequent distribution to retailers. A retailer can order relatively small quantities of products from a wholesaler. Wholesalers have most products readily available for shipment to retailers. In many cases, a wholesaler has an exclusive arrangement with a manufacturer to sell the manufacturer's products in a geographical area, and the retailer has no choice except to buy from the wholesaler designated for the retailer's locale.

If the manufacturer sells products exclusively through wholesalers, the wholesalers act, in effect, as the manufacturer's sales department. Consequently, the wholesaler provides a significant and valuable service to the manufacturer. The wholesaler also provides a significant and valuable service to the retailer in that it enables retailers to buy smaller quantities of goods, and it also keeps the products on hand (stores the products) for immediate shipment.

If the manufacturer also sells directly to retailers, it will be worth your while to at least inquire of the manufacturer whether you can purchase directly. It might be that the quantities that you will need to purchase directly are too large. If that is the case, you will have to purchase through a wholesaler.

Be advised that some manufacturers are fussy about whom they sell to. See the section on Availability in Chapter 1 for elaboration on this point. Expect wholesalers to enforce any restrictions the manufacturer may have on sales to retailers.

Where can you find wholesalers? A good place is in the Yellow Pages (read Chapter 15). The best way, perhaps, is by asking manufacturers.

Understand that wholesaling is a huge business in the US, and many wholesalers are large enterprises with many large retailer customers. Even the minimum quantities you must order to do business with such wholesalers may be too large for you to handle. In other words, you never have any assurance that a particular wholesaler will agree to do business with you until you ask and then make the arrangements.

Factory-Authorized?

There are retailers and others masquerading as wholesalers. In other words, there may be too many middlemen in your supply chain. You want to deal only with factory-authorized wholesalers. Otherwise, the wholesale prices may be too high. Check with the manufacturer to determine whether a wholesaler is factory-authorized or not. See Chapter 15 to find contact information for manufacturers..

The following is a very small sample list of wholesalers that may provide you with an opportunity to acquire some profitable inventory:

Big Lots Wholesale, *http://www.biglotswholesale.com*

Buylink Marketplace, *http://www.buylink.com*

DBL Distributing, *http://dbldistributing.com*

Fine-Line Products, *http://fine-lineproducts.com*

Glaze, *http://www.glazeinc.com*

Made In USA, *http://madeinusa.com*

Maxam's, *http://www.maxamwholesale.com*

Greatrep, *http://www.greatrep.com*

Oriental Trading Company, *http://www.orientaltrading.com,* see
Figure 12.1

It's well beyond the scope of this book to provide a complete list. This
sampler, however, will show you that you can reach legitimate wholesalers via the Web.

Figure 12.1 Oriental Trading Company website. ©2005 Oriental Trading
Company, Inc. All rights reserved.

Make good use of the search engines. Unfortunately, there are thousands of quasi-legitimate or illegitimate wholesalers on the Web. Thus, once you have identified a wholesaler that sells merchandise for your niche, check it out with the manufacturers to determine whether it is factory-authorized.

Wholesale Networks

In many industries, retailers sell at retail but can also act as wholesalers to other retailers. In some such industries, there is a retailers-wholesalers digital network that you may be able to join. By virtue of being on such a network, you can purchase from retailer-wholesalers. You can even become a wholesaler yourself and sell products to other retailers. These networks can be a significant source of inventory.

Unfortunately, these networks are not documented anywhere, nor do they appear in a directory. You will have to discover them yourself industry by industry, if in fact they exist in your industry. Ask around.

Share Inventory

These networks also enable you to share inventory with other retailers. That is, you may be able to buy in bulk in a cooperative effort. Then you can split up the bulk, and each individual retailer acquires inventory presumably at a lower cost.

Exchange Inventory

These networks also enable you to exchange inventory with other retailers as mentioned in Chapter 10. One retailer may be stuck with excess inventory that another retailer would be happy to have. The network enables you to either sell off or acquire such inventory easily and immediately.

Network

What is the network? In some cases, it is just a structured means of communicating with other businesses coupled with a directory of members. Today, the network is likely to be online (i.e., on the Web) where it provides the most convenience to members. In any event, deals are most likely to be made over the telephone.

Mail-Order Wholesalers

Going back many years, certain mail-order wholesalers have advertised and appealed to wannabe retailers operating out of their homes to buy merchandise and resell it via mail order. This has generally been perceived to be a sort of work-at-home-and-get-rich scheme. Although it has likely worked for some people, it probably hasn't worked for most. Our impression of the merchandise that has been available this way is that it has not been unique or high quality.

Such mail-order wholesalers have transferred their appeal to the Web specifically aimed at wannabe eBay retailers. If you are seriously considering doing business with one of these wholesalers, be advised to consider very carefully the inventory that they offer you. It might be that it simply is not worth your time and effort to sell such inventory. Nonetheless, these old mail-order (now online sales) wholesalers are a source of inventory.

Conveniently, this type of wholesaler usually offers drop shipping. You will want to evaluate costs of such drop shipping very carefully. It may prove very expensive.

Drop Shippers

It's not only the old mail-order wholesalers that provide drop shipping. Once you line up a wholesaler, it pays to ask whether they provide drop shipping and what it costs. Since drop shipping is considered in detail in Chapter 7, we will say no more here except to note that drop shipping is well worth your consideration, particularly when it is cost-effective.

Summary

You will likely do most of your inventory acquisition from wholesalers. Read Chapter 5 to be sure you understand the relationship between retailers and suppliers. Then look for wholesalers that can provide you with the inventory you need. Perhaps the best way to find wholesalers is through the manufacturers of the products you intend to sell. In any event, your best bet is to buy from those wholesalers that are factory-authorized.

13

Inventory Services

Inventory services have one goal: to make it easy for you to find appropriate inventory. They can do this several ways. They can provide a directory of suppliers or drop shipping suppliers; you're on your own to make the contact. They can create programming that brings together a variety of suppliers and their products into one access point (e.g., a website). Or they can create programming that matches suppliers and retailers up in a more directed way. These are valuable services, but they're not free. The commercial world is not static; it changes every day. These services must research and continually update all the information they provide to you, and that requires an ongoing effort employing many people. But it sure can save you a ton of time.

Inventory services are just that: services. Somehow, for a low fee, they bring you together with manufacturers or wholesalers that will provide you with inventory. Unfortunately, this is fertile ground for middlemen and scam artists. Look at these services very carefully. Make sure you know what you are paying for the service. If it's a commission or an unknown markup, more than likely a middleman or a scam artist is behind the service, and the service will prove an expensive source of inventory for you.

Auction Management Services

Certain auction management software services provide directories of suppliers and even useful programming. They provide you with a means of identifying and contacting manufacturers or wholesalers that can supply products for your selling niche on eBay.

For example, Andale (*http://andale.com*) is an auction management service that provides its various services in separate modules so you don't have to buy the whole service to get what you need. One of the services is Andale Suppliers, which matches suppliers and retailers. You register and indicate what you're looking for, and the service makes the match. It also enables you to search through lists of suppliers and provides a program to keep your leads organized.

It is certainly worth your while to occasionally survey the dozens of auction management software services that are available to you—there are new ones every year—in order to pick one that matches your retail operations and management style. While doing so, also pay attention as to whether each service offers a directory of suppliers. Such a directory will offer you one more opportunity to find what you are looking for. Read more about auction management services in Chapter 4.

Keep in mind also that some of these auction management services, like Andale, offer their services in modules. That means you may be able to subscribe to a directory of suppliers for a small fee, even though you don't use that particular auction management service.

Stand-Alone Services

Certain services are now available on the Web that purport to match retailers up with products (see Figure 13.1). Many are drop shipping services. Generally speaking, these new services work well because they are on the Web and are powerful, convenient, and profitable to use. Since the drop shipping services are prototypes of stand-alone services, we cover them thoroughly in this section to give you an idea of what stand-alone inventory services can do for you. (Read Chapter 7 for more on drop shipping.)

Figure 13.1 The Doba website. ©2006 Doba All rights reserved.

Prototypes

Drop shipping services provide you access to the wholesale products of major suppliers. These are not just directories of suppliers updated regularly. They are aggregations of suppliers into services for retailers. For instance, Doba (Jeremy's company – successor to Wholesale Marketer) provides you access to over 17 major suppliers and enables you to buy at wholesale and sell on eBay or elsewhere.

These services are for members who pay a periodic membership fee or a setup fee. The suppliers are major wholesalers offering thousands of products, including name-brand merchandise, across a broad range of industries. You choose the products out of a catalog managed online.

Take a look at:

DropshipDesign, *http://dropshipdesign.com*, 10,000 products

Dropship Direct, *http://dropshipdirect.com*, 11,000 products

Online Supplier, *http://onlinesupplier.com*, no claim as to the number of products

Doba, *http://www.doba.com*, claims 100,000 products

All product claims obtained from numbers published on the requisite websites in the fall of 2005.

SMC

Another service, SMC, now online at *http://smcorp.com*, is a holdover from the mail-order business and has limited merchandise.

These drop shipping services provide you with the power of numbers, in effect, by dealing with suppliers that otherwise don't take the time to do business with small retailers. And you typically get product information such as photographs, descriptions, inventory levels, MSRPs (manufacturer's suggested retail prices), wholesale costs, drop shipping fees, and shipping fees.

Some of these drop shipping services keep merchandise in their own warehouses and do the drop shipping themselves. Some even provide Web hosting services and merchant credit card services for your own website. For example, DropshipDesign provides you with everything, even a website product catalog.

However, not all of these services do the actual drop shipping. For instance, Doba deals strictly with suppliers that drop ship. You pick an item in the Doba catalog first (see Figure 13.2). Then you sell the item on eBay. Finally, when the item has been sold, you order it through Doba, which passes your order on to the appropriate drop shipping supplier. Doba's Order Manager not only keeps track of your orders, but also passes on UPS and FedEx tracking numbers that you, in turn, can pass on to your buyers.

Figure 13.2 A Doba website catalog page for coffee makers. ©2006 Doba All rights reserved.

Packaged Services

A drop shipping service is great, but what more do you need? That's a question well beyond the scope of this book and tough to answer in any circumstances. Whenever presented with a package of services, determine whether you need the extra services in the package and whether they're worth the extra cost.

Were you to go to a supplier by yourself, you would either not be accepted as a retail customer or would have to pay high drop-ship wholesale prices. Instead, a drop shipping service rolls you up with its thousands of other members, in effect, to be one large retail customer with each supplier. In doing so, such a service gets better wholesale prices for merchandise and better drop shipping prices. It typically passes these savings on to you and earns money by charging a fee.

In Contrast

Worldwide Brands, a competitor to drop shipping services mentioned above, is simply a directory of drop shipping suppliers. Although it's a valuable directory updated regularly, it leaves you on your own to make contact and negotiate a deal with each drop shipper.

Other Uses

Surprisingly, there are even offline uses for drop shipping services. For example, Doba has members that are offline businesses (physical stores). They use the Doba catalog to supplement the sales in their stores. In other words, they show the catalog to their customers and take special orders. The orders are drop shipped. Dropship Direct also has a special program for physical store owners in which you cannot participate if you don't own a store.

Education

Drop shipping services are in a position to provide training to their members. For instance, on its website, Doba maintains a Help desk and provides a library of Flash tutorials and ebooks (about two dozen) to assist members in making their eBay retail businesses successful. You can also use live chat and email to communicate with Doba's support team to get your questions answered about the service and also about ecommerce issues.

eBay Live

Jeremy has participated in panel discussions at eBay Live, the annual eBay conference, and Clark Winegar, Doba's Director of Product Management, has conducted workshops online for eBay. Doba is a Certified eBay Developer and partners with website development software companies to teach them how to handle a drop shipping service in their software and also to integrate Doba capability into their software.

Dropship Direct sponsors several online forums where you can discuss issues and get help from peers as well as Dropship Direct support.

Opportunity

What's the opportunity here? Well, this is a terrific opportunity for drop shipping suppliers. They don't have to deal with small individual retailers, yet through a drop shipping service, they get a substantial amount of business from one source. That's why drop shipping services have many major suppliers in their fold and why they can offer many products.

The big story, however, is that eBay retailers can get a huge selection of products drop shipped, get the lowest drop-ship wholesale prices and drop shipping fees, and get order management capability as well. What a deal! It doesn't get any easier than this.

A drop shipping service is a particularly good deal for you if you are just starting out and want to get some experience selling before you narrow down your choice of niches, spend a lot of time finding suppliers, and buy the equipment and supplies you will need to do your own fulfillment. Later, when you have a better idea what you want to do long term, you can switch into a normal retailing system. For many, however, a competent drop shipping system will prove a profitable system itself worthy of a long-term commitment.

Directory Services

There are services that are essentially online directories. Why do we call them services? Because they are updated regularly. They are not frozen in print only to be revised annually or less often. With ongoing research, the sponsors update the directories daily or weekly. You pay a subscription fee for access. Check out:

Worldwide Brands, *http://worldwidebrands.com*, see Figure 13.3

Hienote, *http://www.hienotedirectory.com*

What Do I Sell, *http://whatdoisell.com*

Wholesale Central, *http://wholesalecentral.com*

Wholesale Club, a list – *http://wholesaleclub.com*

Also read Chapter 24, which warns you about scam supplier directories and services that are always out of date and worthless.

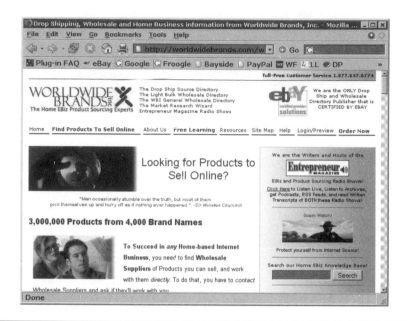

Figure 13.3 Worldwide Brands website. ©2005 Worldwide Brands

eBay

eBay itself offers a category of listings for products—potentially wholesale priced—called Wholesale Lots (*http://pages.ebay.com/catindex/catwholesale.html*). Although every other eBay retailer may be assumed to be using this category, nonetheless it could prove to be a fruitful resource for finding inventory and also suppliers. It's certainly one you will want to investigate. On the eBay homepage go Wholesale Lots to check out these bulk sales for both inventory to purchase at wholesale prices and as a means of identifying suppliers.

Many of these bulk sales are actually closeouts, which may not provide leads to suppliers that will be ongoing sources of inventory. Nonetheless, Wholesale Lots will provide you with a good sense of reality in regard to wholesale pricing and quantities. Read more about closeouts in Chapter 14.

If you're an eBay PowerSeller, you can take part in the new (in 2005) eBay Reseller Marketplace (*http://reseller.ebay.com* – see Figure 13.4). It's a special eBay place for both buyers and sellers to make bulk inventory transactions. It has a lot of promise, but it was just getting off the ground as this book went to press. You will want to check periodically on this potential source of inventory to see how it develops.

Figure 13.4 eBay Reseller Marketplace.

Summary

Inventory services can save you time and money. The nature of inventory services is to bring you together with legitimate suppliers for a relatively small fixed fee. This can save you a lot of time. Moreover, it can save you money. If the inventory service is working for you, it will put you in contact with only legitimate wholesalers that can offer you the lowest wholesale prices.

14

Closeouts

There is a closeout (liquidation, surplus) industry that buys excess merchandise from large retailers, wholesalers, manufacturers, and even the government in bulk for pennies on the dollar and resells it in bulk to retailers for a few more pennies on the dollar. Some closeout vendors sell goods by the warehouse pallet (a 4 ft × 4 ft wooden base piled about 7 feet high with goods), some by the truckload. This is a competitive industry that, like any other industry, requires a lot of hard work for success. Many closeout companies have gone to the Web to sell their goods in bulk to wannabe retailers who think they can sell the goods profitably online (e.g., on eBay). Some closeout companies are even selling in bulk on eBay.

This is a big business that covers liquidations, returns, job lots, off-price lots, overstocks, overruns, surplus, salvage, unclaimed freight, and pallet merchandise. There are closeout shows, newspapers, and magazines.

You must distinguish between merchandise that is all new or "in new condition" and merchandise that is returned, secondhand, or even damaged. There are no guarantees. You get the stuff "as is" (i.e., no returns). So you better ask a lot of questions before you buy. And don't forget to check out the closeout supplier thoroughly too.

Opportunity?

Is this a potential source of inventory for your eBay business? Sure. Do you have to be careful? Yes. In fact, your chances of success in playing the closeout game may be much less than for other sources of acquiring saleable inventory. This is not a source of inventory you want to jump into big time without considerable experience at retailing closeout products. Start small, be careful, and remember that the closeout marketplace is the home of the middlemen. It is also the home of the scam artists.

Sources

Below are some closeout companies and organizations you can investigate (not screened for quality):

- American Merchandise Liquidators, *http://amlinc.com*
- American Science & Surplus, *http://www.sciplus.com*
- AmeriSurplus, *http://amerisurplus.com*
- Closeout, *http://www.closeout.com*
- Closeout Central, *http://www.closeoutcentral.com*
- Closeout Heaven, *http://www.closeoutheaven.com,* see Figure 14.1
- CloseOutNow, *http://www.closeoutnow.com*
- CloseoutServices, *http://www.closeoutservices.com*
- Closeout Warehouse, *http://www.thecloseoutwarehouse.com*
- Commodity Surplus, *http://www.commoditysurplus.com*
- Computer & Electronic Surplus, *http://www.73.com*
- Big Lots Wholesale, *http://biglotswholesale.com*
- Jane's Closeout Marketplace, *http://www.janesdeals.com*
- Dalbani, *http://www.dalbani.com*
- Discount Warehouse, *http://www.closeouts.digiscape.net*

- Lee Howard's Business Inventory Closeout Sources Directory, *http://www.chambec.com/closeout.html*

- Liquidation Connection, *http://www.liquidationconnection.com*

- Liquidation Station, *http://liquidationstation.com*

Figure 14.1 Closeout Heaven website. ©2005 Closeout Heaven LLC

- Merchandise USA (MUSA), *http://merchandiseusa.com*

- Maverick Enterprises, *http://amaverickent.com*

- My Web Wholesaler, *http://mywebwholesaler.com*

- Overstock B2B, *http://www.overstockb2b.com*

- Premier Products International, *http://www.hotbuy4u.com*

- QVC, *http://www.qvc.com*

- RetailExchange, *http://retailexchange.com*

- RLC Trading, *http://rlctrading.com*, where you can find an online tutorial on closeouts, *http://rlctrading.com/101.htm*

- RO-EL On-Line, *http://www.ro-el.com*

- Salvage Closeouts, *http://www.salvagecloseouts.com*
- Sav-On-Closeouts, *http://www.sav-on-closeouts.com*
- Sell 2 All, *http://www.sell2all.com*
- S&M Distributors, *http://www.worldliquidators.net*
- Surplus Hut, *http://www.surplushut.com*
- Surplus Net, *http://surplus.net*
- TDW Closeouts, *http://www.tdwcloseouts.com*
- uBid, *http://www.ubid.com* (see Figure 14.2)

Some of the above may be jobbers or brokers, people (companies) who buy closeouts and resell the closeouts to wholesalers, or even retailers. Beware also that sometimes there is such a long line of middlemen between you and the closeout source that you can't buy a closeout cheap enough to sell the merchandise at a profit.

Local Sources

Note that the closeouts featured on the list above seek a national clientele. If you want to buy closeouts locally and don't want to buy through middlemen, you will need to develop your own local sources.

There are also two publications in which you may find sources of inventory. Try the *Closeout News* and *Wholesale Merchandise*. You can order subscriptions at *http://www.thecloseoutnews.com*.

Also, let's not forget the government. Below is a sample of auctions that may be a fruitful means of finding something to sell:

Department of the Treasury, *http://www.treas.gov/auctions/customs*

General Services Administration (GSA), *http://www.gsa.gov/Portal/gsa/ep/contentView.do?contentId=9881&contentType=GSA_BASIC)*

Services

The closeout organizations below are special in that they have been exhibitors at the eBay Live conference and cater to eBay retailers.

Figure 14.2 uBid website. ©1997-2005 uBid, Inc. All rights reserved.

Liquidity Services Inc. With three websites, this company matches buyers (e.g., eBay retailers) with sellers (closeout manufacturers, wholesalers, and retailers):

Liquidation (*http://www.liquidation.com*) – This online auction features general surplus including state government surplus. It has 20,000 different items for sale at any given time and is updated regularly.

Government Liquidation (*http://www.govliquidation.com*) – This is an auction site for US military surplus. That means all kinds of things. You don't have to be shopping for an F-4 Phantom jet fighter to find stuff here to sell on eBay (see Figure 14.3).

GoWholesale (*http://gowholesale.com*) – This is a search engine that matches eBay retailers (and other retailers) with closeout retailers and wholesalers.

Liquidity's Liquidation and Government Liquidation websites use auctions without reserves to sell the surplus merchandise. The auction mechanisim is similar to eBay, but the rules are a little different. This is a comfortable way for eBay retailers to acquire inventory.

Figure 14.3 Government Liquidation, a closeout website. © 2001-2005 Government Liquidation, LLC., a subsidiary of Liquidity Services, Inc. All rights reserved.

Luxury Brands This is an interesting company. Find it at *http://luxurybrandsllc.com*. It imports closeouts of European clothing and apparel, mostly in small quantities and makes them available to US retailers. This is a popular service, and you have to get on a mailing list in order to be able to purchase their surplus merchandise. Don't dally when you see something you want to buy from Luxury Brands to sell on eBay, or you may be too late (see Figure 14.4).

Figure 14.4 Luxury Brands website.

These look more like services similar to the ones in Chapter 13 than the individual suppliers on the long list above. You are almost certain to have more luck using them.

Case Study

Joe looked for a camera tripod on GoWholesale. Here's what he found in 10 seconds:

53-inch silver camera tripod with bubble level, 360-degree swivel panhead, 90-degree vertical platform, adjustable controls, quick-release platform, gear operated center column, quick-release leg locks, nylon carrying case, new, made in China, packaged in retail box – 10 packaged units in master box – 20 master boxes on each pallet – price for buying 10+ units is $7.88 each

Quantity in stock: 9,490.

Further investigation indicated that this same tripod sells for between $20 and $35 in online discount stores. An eBay retailer sells this routinely on eBay for between $5 and $16. However, the eBay retailer charges a $16 flat fee for shipping and handling. At 2.6 lbs it costs about $6 to ship coast to coast via the US Postal Service. Thus, after the cost of goods and shipping, the eBay retailer is netting between $7 and $18 per item. Dozens are sold each week on eBay by this retailer. (Note the cost of shipment of the tripods from the wholesaler to the eBay retailer was not taken into account in calculating the net.)

The point here is not to say this is a good or bad retailing opportunity. It appears to be one that's working for someone, and Joe was able to find it in just a matter of seconds.

Will They Work?

These services sure look good to us. Joe's casual case study proves that there's plenty of potential for you whether you know exactly what you're looking for or you're just fishing for something to sell profitably.

Learn to Use Closeouts

Even if you don't get involved in the closeout business, learn enough about closeouts to recognize a good deal when you see it. This is a learning process that will take time, effort, and experimentation. And then be ready to take quick action when you run across a potentially profitable closeout from time to time. You don't want to see a good closeout end up in the hands of one of your eBay competitors.

Usually a closeout is a one-time purchase that doesn't necessarily engender a long-term relationship with a supplier. However, there's no inherent reason you can't establish an enduring relationship with a closeout supplier, particularly one that specializes in the type of merchandise that you sell. After all, you want the supplier to come to you first with attractive closeout offers before going to your competitors.

Summary

Closeouts are a potential source of profitable inventory both on a one-time basis and for ongoing acquisitions. But it's not a source for the unwary. Study the closeout industry. Experiment with the smallest quantities possible. Develop some trustworthy sources. Then work closeouts into your inventory acquisition routine. Closeouts can be the frosting on your retail cake.

15

Directories

Directories contain good solid information you can trust and use. Primarily it's information that ultimately enables you to contact a manufacturer or even a wholesaler. This contact at the root of the supply chain is the starting point for determining where you can buy inventory at the lowest possible wholesale price.

Why do you need the contact information for manufacturers if you will spend most of your time dealing with wholesalers? First, a great way to identify legitimate wholesalers is through a manufacturer. Second, the only way to tell if a wholesaler is factory authorized is to check with the manufacturer.

Consequently, directories can play an important role in your ongoing research to find inventory.

Library

Go to your library. Then go to the reference section. Ask the reference librarian where you can get started with finding sources of inventory. He or she may refer you to some of the following just from one publisher, Thomson Gale (*http://www.gale.com*):

American Wholesalers and Distributors Directory

Dun & Bradstreet/Gale Industry Reference Handbooks

Small Business Sourcebook

Ward's Business Directory of U.S. Private and Public Corporations

Thomson Gale also publishes information and data on its website (see Figure 15.1).

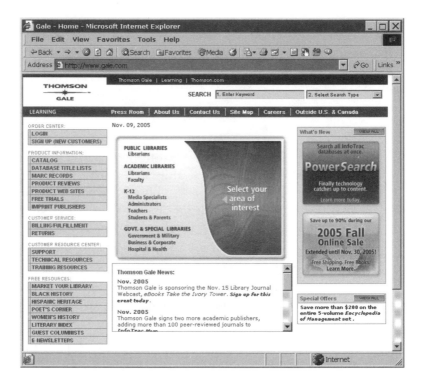

Figure 15.1 Thomson Gale website. ©2005 Thomson Gale, a part of The Thomson Corporation.

Most libraries stock these kinds of references. If you live in a large city, the library may have designated one of its branches as a business library. It will probably be more worth your while to visit that library to find references to manufacturers and wholesalers than to visit a normal library. Such a library is likely to stock more directories.

How to Contact

This is a good technique for finding products if you know the manufacturer or wholesaler but have no way to contact it. This gives you a chance to look up the company's address and telephone listings, which will give you a good start on contacting the person you need to talk with to buy inventory.

You may want to familiarize yourself with the North American Industry Classification System (NAICS). Using NAICS codes may help you identify more easily the manufacturers and wholesalers handling the products you are looking for.

SIC Replacement

NAICS codes replaced Standard Industrial Classification (SIC) codes a few years back, and SIC codes are no longer used.

Harris Infosource (*http://harrisinfo.com*), Twinsburg, OH, publishes many directories that may help you identify manufacturers and wholesalers:

[State]: All Businesses (one for each state)

Complete Guide to NAICS

National Wholesalers and Distributors (also regional editions)

Harris also publishes on CDs and on its website.

Hoover's (*http://www.hoovers.com*), Austin, TX, publishes several directories you will find useful for tracking down companies:

Hoover's Handbooks

Hoover's Master List of Major US Companies

Hoover's also publishes on its website.

McGraw-Hill, Charlottesville, VA, publishes a standard reference for US corporations:

Standard & Poor's Register

Thomas Publishing (*http://www.thomasnet.com*), New York, publishes business resources including:

Thomas Register of American Manufacturers

The *Register* is the definitive directory for industrial companies. Thomas is also a great Web resource for finding industrial product suppliers. You will want to take a thorough look at the ThomasNet website (see Figure 15.2). Publishing products are also available on CDs and DVDs but, like other resources, at prices that will make you appreciate your local library resources.

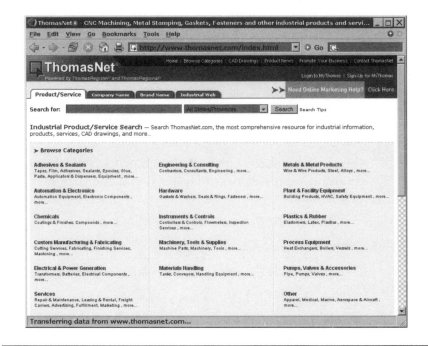

Figure 15.2 ThomasNet industrial website. ©2005 Thomas Publishing Company. All rights reserved.

Again, look for the references above in your library. Few libraries will have all of them, but most libraries will have some of them.

Directories Online

Many of the directories mentioned above have gone online for the obvious reasons. A directory online can be kept up-to-date more easily and less expensively, and users can use it more conveniently. Some of the directories mentioned earlier have disappeared from print because the information is now available on the Web. Some of these directories are free, such as ThomasNet (mentioned earlier). For others, you will have to pay a fee for access. These are terrific references.

Check the Library

What do you do when the librarian says, "No, we don't have those printed directories any longer." Look on the Web.

If a directory charges a fee for access, you may find that your library is a subscriber. You can then use the library computers for free access to the directory.

By virtue of having a library card, you may be able to gain free access to such a directory via the library's network, which you access via the Internet. If a library gives you free access to such a directory via its network, that gives you a great incentive to get a library card. Normally, you use your name and library card number as your login to the library network.

You can use the usual Web search engines to find contact information on manufacturers and wholesalers. Try Google (*http://www.google.com*), Yahoo (*http://search.yahoo.com*), and Altavista (*http://www.altavista.com*).

For instance, try Yahoo and search the Yahoo Directory with the keyword *wholesale*. You can even narrow it down to a local search. It works well. But it doesn't work well using the *Web* search on Google, Yahoo or Altavista.

Specialty Directories and Catalogs Online

There are also directories and catalogs online that specialize in matching manufacturers and wholesalers up with retailers. It's difficult to separate the wheat from the chaff—often quite difficult. When you find such websites, always check out the wholesalers to determine if they are factory authorized (to be assured of getting the lowest possible wholesale prices). Use the directories in this chapter to get contact information for the manufacturers.

Inventory Service

The inventory services covered by Chapter 13 often take the form of online directories of manufacturers and wholesalers. You can browse through a structured list (e.g., alphabetical) or use an online search to find what you're looking for.

Chamber of Commerce

The Chamber of Commerce in each city and town usually prints (or puts online) a directory of businesses that are members. You can learn a lot about where you live by reviewing such a directory published by your local chamber. You may discover potential sources of inventory you didn't know existed locally.

Figure 15.3 Peoria Area Chamber of Commerce website, Peoria, Illinois. ©2005 Peoria Area Chamber of Commerce

Yellow Pages

Perhaps the best known directory of all is the Yellow Pages. While the Yellow Pages directories are published by various companies, the one that remains one of the best is the one published by the telephone company. If you need to find a wholesaler, this may be a good place for you to start. In fact, if you're in a large city, this may be an excellent resource for you to find inventory at a wholesale cost.

Where do you look? Just look up businesses that sell products. Normally there will be both retail and wholesale listings and sometimes manufacturer listings.

Wholesalers and even manufacturers often advertise in the Yellow Pages even in outlying towns and cities where they do not have an office or warehouse. Therefore, even in a small city directory or a small town directory, you may be able to find resources for products that will suit your retail sales. Since this is a resource that's likely to be right under your nose—and free—use it!

Summary

If you can trace a product that you want to sell to a manufacturer, you can find the manufacturer in a directory and get its contact information. At that point, getting inventory is just a few telephone calls away. If you know the general category into which a product falls, you may be able to find a wholesaler in the Yellow Pages or another directory. With a telephone number, again, getting inventory is just a telephone call away. Finding sources of inventory doesn't have to be difficult or complicated. It can be as easy as finding a directory.

16

Picking

"Picking" is just a fancy name for shopping. But it's shopping with a purpose. A picker goes shopping, buys something, and sells it to a retailer for a small markup. In other words, picking is a service. The way this chapter treats picking is as if you, the retailer, were doing it. In reality, you can do it yourself, or you can find an independent contractor (someone working on their own for a small markup) to do it. You might even have an employee do it. But whoever does it, picking simply amounts to finding and buying merchandise that you can acquire at a low price and sell on eBay at a high price.

General Marketplace Picking

Picking is well-known in the antiques business. Antique shops pay people to go out and find antiques in various places. The so-called pickers go to private homes, garage sales, local auctions, and other places where antiques might be found and buy individual antiques. They then bring them into the antique shop and sell them to the antique shop owner for a profit. This is a way for pickers to make a few bucks and a way for antique shops to acquire inventory.

You can do the same. You don't have to limit your picking to antiques.

You can go out picking for collectibles, cameras, electronic equipment, and other items that are profitable to acquire at a cheap price and sell for a profit on eBay. What you are likely to find is the antique pickers are now selling their antiques on eBay rather than to antique shops. And there are plenty of pickers picking away in your locale for items to sell on eBay.

Yes, there's competition. Nonetheless, if your retail operation is one that requires picking, get out there and compete. Picking can be a very profitable way to acquire inventory.

Retail Picking

A common eBay business, particularly among women, is to pick designer clothes where they can find them inexpensively (e.g., factory outlet malls). They then sell such clothing on eBay at higher prices. Although this is a popular part-time retail business with some women, there's no reason you can't make it a full-time retail business, as many do.

But don't think designer clothes are the only opportunity. Wholesale outlets such as Costco (*http://www.costco.com* – see Figure 16.1) and Sam's Club (*http:// samsclub.com*) often buy huge quantities of products and pass very low prices along to their customers. They even feature occasional closeouts at especially low prices. Usually these closeout products are only available for a short time because such wholesale retailers are very good at moving product quickly. Thus, when such an offering appears, you can buy such products in bulk and start selling them for higher prices on eBay.

You might want to wait to start selling until the discount store runs out of product, but that probably won't be necessary. Not everybody shops at discount stores every week, but everybody likes to buy at a bargain.

For instance, a few years ago when DVD players were new and sold at no less than $160, Joe found them for sale in a closeout at Costco for $90. Supply lasted only about a week, but it provided a window of opportunity for an alert eBay retailer to buy a quantity of these name-brand DVD players and sell them on eBay for a quick profit. If this source of inventory appeals to you, you will need to visit the discount stores often so as not to miss one of these temporary offerings.

Figure 16.1 Costco website. ©1998-2005 Costco Wholesale Corporation.
All rights reserved.

A discount store doesn't have to be a huge chain like Costco. Try Tuesday Morning (*http://www.tuesdaymorning.com*) or other less well-known chains. And don't forget the factory outlet malls.

A low-end genre of discount stores (dollar stores) specializes in selling at retail the inventory acquired from closeouts, overruns, small runs, and out-of-date merchandise. They are present in many communities. Most of them sell only low-cost merchandise, but it might be worthwhile to check them out. Here's a partial list:

Dollar Discount (*http://www.dollardiscount.com*)

Dollar Store (*http://www.dollarstore.com*)

Dollar Tree (*http://www.dollartree.com*)

Family Dollar (*http://familydollar.com*)

It may also be worthwhile for you to check out the dollar store warehouses in order to buy direct.

Other Picking

When you're an eBay retailer, just going out shopping can be a picking-like experience. This is particularly true when you shop in a place where you can acquire products in bulk at low prices such as Costco.

It's also true when you shop in a place where you may come across new products in your industry such as at a specialty store. Although a specialty store is not likely to sell you the products at wholesale, at least through your shopping you will be alerted to new products that you might want to stock.

Cost

The nice thing about picking is that you can not only acquire products at a low cost but also avoid shipping costs from suppliers. Thus, at a local Costco closeout sale, you may be able to acquire inventory at a price below wholesale and without the additional expense of paying for shipping. This is an important technique of acquiring inventory to keep in mind, if appropriate for your retail business.

Beyond Your Own Picking

Picking is not just for you personally. As mentioned earlier, you can use pickers. They are like employees who go out to find and buy inventory for you—except you don't have to pay them! You make payment only when they find and buy something you can sell at a profit.

If picking is right for your eBay retail business, leverage your time. Get a group of pickers working for you. Don't take this technique lightly. Get organized. Make an effort to keep in cell phone contact with your pickers so that they can contact you easily when they find something. Be ready to make a quick trip, if necessary, to look over the item for the picker prior to a purchase. Be prepared to pay your pickers upon delivery—in cash. Treat them fairly financially so that they don't go picking for one of your competitors.

Summary

Some retail businesses require picking, such as the antique business. Yet this isn't an idea that has limitations. For used items, and even for new merchandise, picking is good business. You can get a start on your eBay retailing by picking yourself. When successful, you can recruit others to pick for you. This is a simple technique that you may find well worthwhile if it fits your business.

17

Local Sources

Local sources are extremely valuable. Communication is easy, particularly one-to-one, in-person communication, which is always the best (e.g., you can get in your car and go talk with a supplier). You can potentially save money on supplier-retailer shipping, and you can network more easily than you can from afar. But oddly enough, local sources are often overlooked by wannabe eBay retailers looking for the elusive eBay retail "secrets." There are no eBay retail secrets. There's just a lot of work to be done in finding inventory. And one of the best places to start looking is right in your own locale, as mundane as that might sound. Hey, maybe this qualifies as a secret. Don't tell anyone.

Excess Retail

Local merchants often have excess merchandise that they put on sale at the end of the season. Sometimes they have a huge amount of excess merchandise to sell off. This presents a good opportunity for you to go in and negotiate a good price to buy such inventory for your eBay retail business.

How does this differ from a local closeout? A local closeout is usually a huge amount of goods that a local retailer has taken the trouble to package (i.e., put on a pallet) and present for sale to people who buy closeouts. Chapter 14 covers closeouts.

The idea of excess inventory is one that requires you to visit local retailers and find out what excess inventory they are willing to sell to you. This opportunity to acquire inventory is most often a seasonal opportunity, as much merchandise is sold on a seasonal basis. Therefore, you might want to approach local merchants time and time again on a seasonal basis to see what they have to offer you. After a few years of doing so, you might find that they will contact you.

For instance, Joe knows a woman who goes to season-end sales at major shopping centers. Her husband travels in a three-state region on business, and she accompanies him to visit the local malls. She is able to pick up enough inventory at low prices for almost full-time selling on eBay. She is not shy about negotiating intensely with department store managers to get the best prices on her volume purchases.

Newspaper Classified Ads

Just like the Yellow Pages is an obvious source of acquiring inventory locally, so is the classified ads section of your local newspaper. Nonetheless, it's one that must be mentioned because it has a lot of potential, particularly for certain types of products. Yes, people still do use the newspaper classifieds to sell certain kinds of things, and when you're looking for products to buy at a low price and sell at a high price, newspaper classifieds might be useful to you.

Many newspapers have now put their classifieds online. In fact, chains of newspapers have put their classifieds online in one Web location. This enables you to go in and find items at one website for numerous newspapers. This is a convenience factor that makes this technique much more powerful than just going through your local classified ads in your local newspaper.

Sale Places

There are local sales all around you that can be sources of your eBay inventory. For example:

Shop the garage sales. This is another obvious I-don't-need-a-book-to-tell-me-this kind of technique. It is certainly not a technique which fosters the ongoing acquisition of enough inventory for a particular niche. But for people who are selling a variety of used products, this source may be worthwhile. And if it isn't worthwhile for you, why not engage a picker? Find someone that likes to go to garage sales and give them the criteria for products that you desire them to buy. When they bring you the products, buy the products and sell them on eBay.

Flea markets (swaps and exchanges) are similar to garage sales in that the pickings may be slim. Nonetheless, it's a source worth trying if the potentially available merchandise fits your retail business. Try the following for locations:

National Flea Market Association (*http://fleamarkets.org*)

Swapmeets (*http://swapmeets.com*)

Estate sales can be very productive. Someone dies. The relatives don't want the stuff; they want money. A probate attorney hires a professional to sell off the stuff. And you go to the sale and spot some bargains. Give it a try.

Thrift Stores

Thrift stores carry general used merchandise much of which is good quality. Goodwill, the Salvation Army, and others can be an ongoing source of inventory for some eBay retailers. You can even shop the Goodwill online (*http://shopgoodwill.com*). The prices are generally low, enabling you to potentially make a profit when you sell.

Auctions

Auctions can serve a lot of purposes from liquidations to getting rid of abandoned stuff in storage units. Although we all think that auctions are a good source of products to buy and then sell on eBay, few people have ever been to a local auction. Local auctions, run by professional auctioneers, can indeed be a good source of inventory to sell on eBay. But in order to make this a viable technique for acquiring inventory, you do have to attend some auctions to see whether they will work for you.

There are two problems with auctions today. First, local auctioneers are auctioning some stuff on eBay these days rather than doing it in local live auctions. Thus, if you are a local auctioneer, and doing a good job for your clients, you will auction off such items on eBay that can get the best prices on eBay, and you will auction off the other items at a local live auction (i.e., the items that will get a better price at a live auction).

Second, local auctioneers often use eBay as a guide to set the beginning prices for things that they auction locally. This practice certainly has the potential for eliminating the opportunity for profitability for you. As you can see, these developments in the auctioneering business resulting from eBay's effective national marketplace tend to make local auctions a potential dead-end for acquiring inventory at a good price.

Everything said above about local auctions, however, assumes a perfect world. The world is not perfect. Consequently, local auctions remain a potential source of inventory for retail sales on eBay. We don't know what is happening in your community, and only you can find out. You may find that local auctions are a dry well, or you may find that local auctions are a reasonable source of inventory for you. The only way you will find out is to attend a few auctions. Get your name on the mailing lists of local auctioneers.

Here are a few tips for attending an auction:

- Get there early to check out the stuff.
- Set your high bid limits, and don't get caught up in the excitement.
- Have cash with you unless you've arranged for payment otherwise.
- Carry your sales tax license.
- Be ready to take possession and cart away immediately.
- Carry inspection tools (e.g., magnifying glass, magnet, etc.).
- Keep to the back of the room so you can see the other bidders.
- Stay calm and pay attention.

These tips assume you know how to bid. If not, learn ahead of time. These tips also assume you know the jargon pertaining to the stuff being auctioned. If not, you'd better learn ahead of time.

Liquidations

This is a catch-all category that covers everything from local liquidation auctions to going-out-of-business sales. Local liquidations are common and may be an opportunity to pick up inventory at wholesale prices or below. You can find them noticed or advertised in your local newspaper. Stay alert.

Point of Interest Gift Shops

Gift shops in museums, national parks, exotic towns, etc., sell unique products, primarily souvenir items. They sell only locally, yet the products may have national appeal. If you have something of that sort in your town, you may be able to sell its souvenirs or other products on eBay.

For instance, fudge is a primary product of Mackinac Island, Michigan, a grand old summertime tourist location. The fudge is unique and very tasty. Sure, you can get it a few other places around the country, but usually stale. If you live on Mackinac Island or in one of the nearby mainland towns, why not make arrangements with one of the many sources on the island to get it wholesale (and fresh) and then sell it on eBay? Oddly enough, when Joe checked, no one was selling it on eBay. It is sooooo good!

Other Online Marketplaces

You also might want to check Google or Froogle to see if it is sold there before you commit yourself to selling. (In this case, Joe found shops in Mackinac Island via Google where you can order the fudge online. There was nothing on Froogle.)

How about bullfight posters from Monterrey, Mexico? Joe found none on eBay, none on Google, and none on Froogle. Yet the Plaza de Toros in this city of three million is a major attraction. Do these posters have a national appeal in the United States? Who knows? Bullfight posters from Spain sell very well.

And what about a T-shirt from Hell, Michigan?

Craig's List

eBay has never quite figured out how to do local auctions effectively. Craig's List has created very active local marketplaces in over 100 cities both in the US and abroad. Craig's List has outflanked the local classified ads in many of the cities in which it now has a presence. Therefore, Craig's List is an excellent place to find inventory that can be purchased inexpensive locally and sold for a profit on eBay.

This does not happen automatically. It depends on individual markets, individual products, and the way such products are sold. But there's certainly a lot of potential for finding some inventory. So don't overlook Craig's List.

eBay & Craig's List

eBay acquired a 25 percent ownership in Craig's List in the summer of 2004.

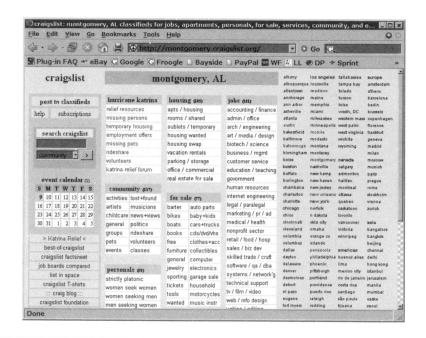

Figure 17.1 Craig's List Montgomery, Alabama. ©2005 Craigslist, Inc.

Partnership

There may be a huge source of inventory staring you right in the face that you don't recognize. You may have retail businesses in your community that have excess inventory to sell on an ongoing basis or that want to start selling their inventory aggressively online. But the owners are not computer literate, and they don't have the time to master the skills and knowledge that it takes to sell online and on eBay effectively and profitably.

Go to them with a business plan that outlines selling their merchandise on eBay. They provide and carry the merchandise and pay the modest overhead bills. You sell the merchandise on eBay and handle the shipping and customer service.

This can be a mutually beneficial way of starting an eBay retail business without having to worry about acquiring and carrying inventory. That is, you can keep capital requirements for your eBay business close to zero.

What kinds of arrangements you make with a local retailer are up for negotiation. But if you are a true entrepreneur, you will propose this as a partnership arrangement rather than trying to become an employee. *There are plenty of local retail stores that have gone out of business because they did not go online and establish a substantial online sales effort.* Many will follow the same path in the future if they don't establish profitable sales online. It's up to you to identify such retail businesses and go to one with a business plan.

Summary

Our experience is that many new and old eBay retailers look everywhere but close to home to find inventory. Don't overlook your own locale. You may find opportunities you never dreamed of to get inventory just by doing a thorough survey of what's available. Leave no rock unturned in your local quest. Local sources are particularly appealing when found because they are usually convenient. Do your homework.

18

Arts and Crafts

The local artists and craftspeople are a potential source of inventory in every sizable community, and even in small communities in exotic locations that seem to attract more than their share of such people. This is an unusual source of inventory in that you are likely to deal with one-person businesses rather than companies (e.g., manufacturers and wholesalers). Consequently, it takes a personal touch to make the best of this source. But what great fun! You can provide a service to artists and craftspeople while at the same time bring their unique and appealing products to marketplaces online.

Keep in mind that for this sort of retailing, the customer service extends in both directions: to the suppliers as well as the buyers. This type of retailing isn't the easiest, but it's one of the most fulfilling.

The Difference

What's the difference between arts and crafts? We are going to stick our neck way out here and attempt to paint two stereotypes, which will give you a glimpse of whatever difference exists between artists and craftspeople. The pictures we will paint of each, of course, are not uniformly true. Nonetheless, they're worth considering because they will make you sensitive to the attitudes of the people with whom you must deal to acquire inventory.

Artists

A typical successful artist who is able to make his or her living by selling art is likely to be talented and well-educated. Each work of art he or she turns out is unique. There are some exceptions to this, of course, such as numbered prints. But often an artist's product is a unique product, not a mass-manufactured product. The price of art objects tends to be higher than the price of craftworks. Art objects also have little function other than their aesthetic value. In other words, art objects are more than decorative; they demand an aesthetic, intellectual, and emotional response from viewers.

Certainly there are artists who are superb businesspeople. But good artists in general don't tend to have business acumen as their forte. They would rather create their art than market it. Consequently, they are a potential source of products for you to sell on eBay.

Many artists have to attend art shows to sell their art. This means traveling widely, with huge allotments of time devoted to marketing and selling rather than creating new works of art.

Often the only alternative is selling at retail, usually through galleries. When you talk to artists about selling at retail, you will invariably hear them complain that they don't get full price for their works of art even when they are delighted to have their works sold at retail. They seem to resent that often retailers make just as much for selling products at retail as manufacturers do for manufacturing the products. Artists don't like to see themselves as manufacturers or be compared to manufacturers.

For that reason, when you try to make an arrangement to sell an artist's art, you will need to tread lightly. A business negotiation to determine the wholesale price is often a very sensitive one. In fact, art in galleries is typically sold on a consignment basis.

A consignment sale is a good deal for both the artists and the retailers (e.g., gallery owners). When a sale is made, it gives the artist a larger percentage of the purchase price. And since the gallery owner did not have to pay for the painting, the gallery owner's risk is less.

The selling risk for most works of art by most artists is substantial indeed. You will probably find that if you use a consignment arrangement when dealing with artists, you will be able to acquire inventory more readily with less risk.

Craftspeople

Craftspeople tend to be businesspeople. They are, in effect, small manufacturers. The goods they create are often functional or decorative. Indeed one can find crafts sold in many retail stores, particularly gift shops.

For instance, a nicely varnished small wooden frame for a mirror with hooks at the bottom intended to hold keys is an object that you would expect to find hung close to the front or back door of a house. You enter the house and hang your keys on this object on the wall. (Joe has a similar object by his front door that his wife uses everyday.) The craftsperson who made this particular product is likely to have made this product in volume. Perhaps she crafted a half a dozen of them. Perhaps she made 10 dozen of them. They are decorative yet functional.

A craftsperson is likely sell these objects at arts and craft shows around the country. But such a craftsperson is also likely to sell such products to gift shops or other retail outlets that carry craftworks. In doing so, the craftsperson sells to retailers at a wholesale price and fully expects the retailer will mark up the price to a retail price. If such a craftsperson sells to retailers, it is also likely that the craftsperson will sell to you at wholesale for your subsequent sales on eBay.

You'll find that a lot of craftspeople, just as other people in the general population, do not understand eBay, do not understand computers, or do not want to take the time and effort to market their products on eBay. They would rather spend their time in production than in marketing.

Recently Jeremy met a craftsman who is a great example of the opportunities available with craftspeople. At a crafts fair in Arizona, Jeremy met a man who manufactures all sorts of sports figures out of spare metal gears, sprockets, and parts. He welds them together into ingenious shapes creating craftworks that could complement the sales of many types of sporting goods and sports collectibles.

This man does not actively sell his products on the Web. He supplies a few small retailers and sells his craftworks at crafts fairs. His products are unique and attractive, however, and very likely could be sold profitably on eBay. In fact, he told Jeremy that one company was already selling these craftworks successfully on its website.

Thus, craftspeople provide you with a significant opportunity to acquire inventory for sale on eBay. If the craft market appeals to you, craftspeople can become a significant source of products for you to sell profitably.

You Can't Match Their Price

A craftsperson might already sell their products themselves on eBay. If so, you'll want to make sure they're not selling their products on eBay at their wholesale prices (the prices to you). Otherwise they will be competing with you at prices you obviously can't match.

Marketing and Selling

Why would artists and craftspeople want to do business with you? Because many of them do not like marketing or selling and would rather devote their time to making their products. This inclination creates an opportunity for you to come in and provide the marketing and sales necessary to make their creative endeavors financially successful.

Craft Shows

Where can you find craftspeople? You can find them at local and national craft shows or arts and craft shows. Many locales also have an arts and crafts center where arts and crafts are sold flea-market-style on certain weekends or at certain times of the year. Selling arts and crafts is often an event, and a visit to your local chamber of commerce may provide you with the information you need to attend such events.

Look for arts and craft shows at:

Festival Network Online, *http://festivalnet.com,* see Figure 18.1

Google (directory), *http://directory.google.com/Top/Arts/Visual_Arts /Resources/Events*

Yahoo (directory), *http://dir.yahoo.com/Arts/Events/Festivals*

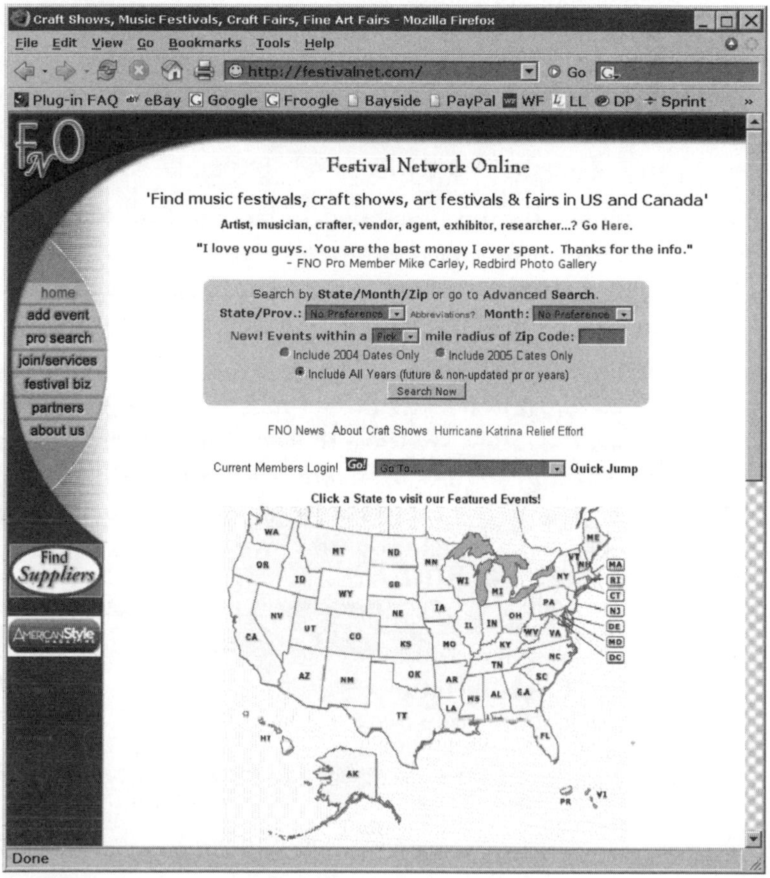

Figure 18.1 Festival Network Online website.

Art Shows

You can find artists at arts and craft shows, and even craft shows. These are usually artists who don't have as much talent and skill as artists who stick strictly to art shows. Arts and craft shows and craft shows are typically not exclusive. Consequently, any artist or craftsperson can become an exhibitor (seller).

Top artists are unlikely to exhibit and sell their art objects at an arts and craft show or a craft show. They are much more likely to sell at an art show. Good art shows tend to be exclusive.

Indeed, the best art shows are juried. That means that a jury of artists and other knowledgable people (judges) looks at the art objects of each artist who applies to be in the show. Only the best artists are admitted. With that in mind, if you are favorably disposed to selling art on eBay, juried art shows are your best bet to make contact with good artists.

Galleries (offline) are logical places to find the works of good artists too. Once you have identified good artists, you can do a little research to find out their contact information (e.g., use the Web). Then you can contact them about selling their art on eBay.

Selling good art is risky, and eBay may not be the best place to do it. In this book, however, we do not judge the likelihood of profitability and success on eBay. We leave that to you. Rather, we simply endeavor to alert you to sources of inventory. Thus, although we believe selling good art on eBay may be a tough sale, if you are so inclined to do it, this chapter will help you find inventory.

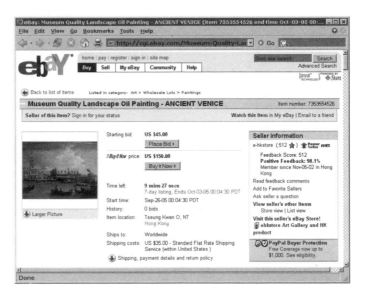

Figure 18.2 Art on eBay. ©1995-2005 eBay Inc. All rights reserved.

People

Remember that when pursuing artists and craftspeople, you are pursuing people. It takes a lot of attempts to find good relationships. Persistence in approaching people will eventually pay off. Building good business relationships requires time and effort. You are not dealing with employees, a staff, a sales force, or a corporate bureaucracy.

Summary

Artists and craftspeople are small manufacturers in your town or city. Many do not like to market their works. This provides you with an opportunity to get inventory for eBay retail sales. Whether you buy this inventory at wholesale or get it on consignment, you will be able to take your local artists and artisans national on eBay.

19

Packages

While not a source of inventory by itself, packaging is a technique for increasing the number and variety of products that you can sell in one sale with the objective of providing customer service as well as making more profit. In other words, it's a good deal for your customers, and it's a good deal for you. It's simply the idea of selling a primary product together with complementary products, or even selling two or more primary products together.

This is not a giveaway technique. It's more trouble for you. Packages don't assemble themselves. This is a profit-making endeavor that enables you to sell inventory that you otherwise would likely not sell.

Accessories

A logical choice of merchandise to package with a product is accessories. That is, additional products that are necessary or desirable to use the primary product effectively. Perhaps the most obvious example is in the digital camera business. A camera retailer wants to sell a camera but also a number of camera accessories in the same sale. And to use a camera effectively, a person usually needs a minimal number of accessories. Therefore, a camera retailer is only too happy to offer you a package (kit) rather than just a camera. Indeed, many people who buy cameras do buy the package.

The potential for extra profits here are often very significant. For instance, the margin on a name-brand product may be 40 percent. The margins on the accessories that you sell along with the camera in a package may be 60 percent, 70 percent, 80 percent, or more. (Remember from Chapter 5, an 80 percent margin is a 400 percent markup.) So the potential for additional profit is considerable. Thus, if you are looking for inventory, look to the accessories that you can sell together with the products that you're already selling. Particularly keep in mind creating packages that will appeal to consumers.

Assembling

What is the cost of creating a package? It's not free. If you are to sell a package, you will have to research products that are available to sell in the package, you will have to acquire those products, and you will have to assemble them into a package once you receive them in inventory. Accordingly, there's work to be done in order to create packages that will appeal to consumers. Thus, you must be careful in your cost-effectiveness evaluation when you speculate that selling packages will be profitable for you.

Bundling

Bundling is a type of packaging. The major difference between assembling and bundling is the cost of the products you assemble into the package to supplement your main product. For instance, when you assemble camera accessories into a package to be sold with a camera, you simply buy those accessories from normal wholesale sources and add them to the package at the desired margins.

When you bundle merchandise with a product you sell, the manufacturer has a serious interest in promoting such bundling merchandise. The manufacturer looks to your sale of your product as an opportunity to promote its own merchandise by providing, in effect, a free sample. Therefore, the manufacturer is willing to provide you useful bundling merchandise for a small fraction of the normal wholesale price.

Figure 19.1 Camera package on eBay. ©1995-2005 eBay Inc. All rights reserved.

For example, this is a typical arrangement in the digital industries. When you buy a digital camera, you're likely to receive a significant amount of software bundled with the camera. Some of the software might actually be trial software which gives consumers a limited time to use it. But often the software has no limitation and can be very useful to consumers. Often it's a watered-down version of a program that provides more robust functionality. In this case, the software manufacturer is betting that even though you get the watered-down version of the software free, you will be willing to pay for the more robust version of the software.

What do digital camera manufacturers pay software developers to bundle software with their cameras? Typically, they pay from five cents to $1.50 to get software to bundle with a digital camera. Retail prices for such software may be anywhere from $29 to $729. Bundling can even be free.

Does bundling work only with digital products and software? No. Bundling works wherever a manufacturer is aggressively promoting merchandise or where you can make the case to a manufacturer that bundling will cost-effectively promote its merchandise. Therefore, bundling is only limited by your imagination.

Keep in mind, however, that the bundling merchandise is not going to come from normal wholesale sources. You will have to seek out manufacturers and make deals.

It could be that there are no bundling opportunities in your retail business. On the other hand, it could be that there are great bundling opportunities that a little imagination and research will uncover. Remember that bundling enables you to provide additional products to your customers at a nominal cost to you.

For Retailers?

Is bundling really for retailers? If your sales volume is sufficient, you can start talking with manufacturers about bundling deals. Naturally, they usually want the widest exposure possible. If your sales volume is low, you probably won't garner much interest from manufacturers. But it doesn't hurt to ask.

Combination

If you combine the techniques of assembling and bundling you may be able to create a very appealing package that consumers just can't resist. These are two powerful ideas, and there's no reason they can't be combined. On the one hand, you're looking for low-cost, high-margin accessories from normal wholesale channels. On the other hand, you are looking for merchandise you can add to the package at a nominal cost that a manufacturer perceives will go a long way toward promoting the merchandise.

Related Products

You can also assemble related products, that is, products that go together but are not necessarily accessories to one another. For instance, let's take the camera example above a little further. Were you to include a book on photography in an assembled package, that's a normal camera accessory. But what if you included a book on *aesthetics* (the theory of beauty)? That's a philosophy book. Sure it's related. After all, we all try to take beautiful photographs. Nonetheless, it's hardly a book that would have wide appeal. Your consumer target market would need to be highly educated people who are art lovers.

What if you included a book on the history of St. Augustine in the assembled package? Well, St. Augustine, Florida, is the oldest city in the US and one of the most charming. It has an old Spanish fort, other old buildings, a tall lighthouse, and the Alligator Farm (which is also a bird sanctuary besides being an alligator and crocodile zoo). St. Augustine is a photographer's paradise. Indeed, it's a destination city for photographers. (Many professional wildlife photographers get their bird shots at the Alligator Farm.) So the book is related. However, your consumer target market would need to be people desiring to travel to Florida.

Summary

There are two assembling techniques for packaging. One focuses on accessories for the general market, and the other focuses on related products for special markets. Your opportunities are only limited by your imagination. And don't overlook bundling if you can arrange it with manufacturers.

What's the point? More products. Greater sales. More profit. And packages intelligently created can be a real benefit to your customers.

20

Special Products

A special product can be anything that's unique and is likely not to be available except for your efforts in making it available (i.e., selling it). This covers a lot of territory, and we implore you not to let this chapter with its limited examples hold back your imagination. The fact is that the public is hungry for unique and appealing products—things that are different. If you can come up with something, you may have a profitable winner on your hands.

Special products require special efforts beyond normal retailing tasks. As such, most special products are most likely to be mass-produced products sold in volume, not one-offs.

Television and Magazine Specials

You've seen those products advertised on television. They're usually $19.95. And they come with accessories or other products at no additional cost. All you have to do is dial 800-123-4567 right now, and you can get an amazing appliance.

What's the primary characteristics of these products? Usually, it's that they are not sold in stores. In fact, they tend to be clever and appealing products that you can only buy on television. Since you can't buy them in your local stores, the only way you know how to buy them is by calling in your order immediately.

You see magazine ads that offer the same thing. The products are not available in stores. Consequently, you have to buy these clever products through the magazine ad.

Wow! This provides you with the potential opportunity to sell spiffy products on eBay that one cannot get in the local stores. What a great deal! The only catch is you have to find the source of the product and make a deal to sell it.

This may take considerable research on your part. If you call in to order the product, the company taking the orders is likely to be a telemarketing service. The person with whom you talk will probably not know any more about the company that makes or markets the product than you do. Thus, you have your work cut out for you. Certainly, many of the resources mentioned in this book may help you find the manufacturer, wholesaler, or person who is providing the product via television or through magazines.

The library and the Internet are two excellent places to start your research. Another place may be through a directory of advertising and marketing agencies that have a hand in these kinds of marketing promotions.

Once you've found the company or person, make the contact, and then make the deal. The company or person in charge of the promotion may want to keep the selling of such product exclusive or may be delighted to develop additional markets for the product. You'll never know unless you ask. If you reach the company or person that manufactures the product and they don't have an exclusive arrangement with a marketing organization, you may be able to make a deal to sell the product on eBay.

Try Glaze (*http://www.glazeinc.com* – see Figure 20.1), a wholesale source for some of the television products.

Manufacture It

If you want to sell a product that you cannot find and it's not to your knowledge manufactured, you may have to manufacture it yourself.

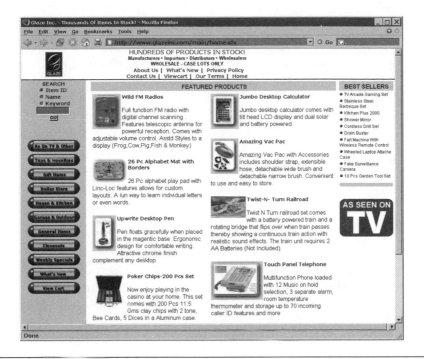

Figure 20.1 Glaze website.

Here you run into patent considerations. If it's an invention, you are well-advised to attempt to patent it before you sell it. If it's just a remake of a common item or of a patent that has expired, you will not have to worry about this.

The biggest drawback to this approach for acquiring inventory is that having something manufactured for you in a factory usually requires large runs (production volume) to be financially feasible on a cost-per-item basis. That means you may have to warehouse a large number of the products, and you will have to have the money (capital) to carry the inventory. Nonetheless, there's plenty of opportunity here for creating products that have the potential of selling well on eBay. You may even want to manufacture a product in your garage.

Special-order manufacturing, which is quite common, is a variant of this idea and is covered in Chapter 11. It is simply the special-order customization of mass-produced products.

One-Person Manufacturer

Joe knows a person who manufactures small, portable tables with folding legs. In fact, Joe uses one to write on his laptop computer while traveling. These tables are made out of particle board with Formica on each side. Rubber molding is fastened around the edge. The table is held up by aluminum legs. The aluminum legs are connected to the tabletop with special plastic fixtures invented by the person doing the manufacturing. The legs are riveted into these plastic fixtures, and the plastic fixtures are screwed to the particle board.

Thus, as you can understand, this is a small table manufactured with off-the-shelf components. The only unique component is the fixture holding the legs to the table, and that is the only component that needs to be mass produced in a factory.

The assembly process is straightforward. The one-person manufacturer simply cuts the tabletop from a larger board, cuts the legs from standard aluminum tubing, rivets the legs to the plastic fixtures, and attaches the fixtures to the tabletop with screws. The person offers several different standard-sized tables with three different heights. You can even have a table custom manufactured for a cost that is close to the cost of the standard tables.

Tables such as these are hard to find for those who travel and need to work on a laptop with comfortable ergonomics (i.e., just the right height). As a result, there is a ready market for this home-manufactured product, and eBay is a cost-effective way to reach such a market. Keep in mind that although this particular one-person operation must have the plastic fixtures made in a factory thousands at a time, he uses four for each table. All the other components are easily purchased locally as needed.

Haven't we all invented something at one time or another that we thought would be a big hit on the retail market? eBay provides you with a golden opportunity to prove your notion. If you can carry the manufacturing costs for special components and build the product with off-the-shelf components readily available locally, you may have yourself a profitable eBay retail business.

Of course the example cited is just one simple situation where you may be able to create your own product. There are thousands of other situations where you may be able to manufacture a profitable product where none of the parts are specially manufactured by someone else. In other words, all the components are off-the-shelf. The sky's the limit on what you can do with this idea.

Normal Manufacturing

OK, so you don't want to manufacture anything. We don't blame you. Have a manufacturer do it. This is what most retailers do who sell specially made products.

Suppose you are the one-person manufacturer above. Your business is so good that you have to spend more time on marketing, selling, and managing. You don't have time to do the manufacturing any longer. It will be easy for you to find a manufacturer that will make the portable tables for you at a reasonable price. The biggest problem you will face is the size of the volume required to get the reasonable price per table. This is a financial problem. You will need the capital necessary to carry the large volume of products until you can sell them all.

When you find an opportunity to manufacture something, don't back away from it just because it seems crazy for a retailer to even think of such a thing. Investigate it. Talk to manufacturers about it. Get cost estimates.

Small manufacturers abound. There are thousands around the US. With a little research, you can find a company to make almost anything for you. But it always gets down to the cost (the cost of the products and the cost to carry them stored until you can sell them) to determine whether special manufacturing is feasible for your retail sales.

Demanufacturing

What the heck is demanufacturing? It's simply taking used products that you can acquire cheap and stripping them down to sell the parts. In other words, the sales prices of the parts are substantially greater than the cost of the used product.

Joe knows a person who is buying used motor scooters in Italy, importing them, and stripping them down for parts to sell to US users of Italian motor scooters. Now there's a niche idea that's not going to support a hundred different competing businesses on eBay. But it might support several. And it's clear at the present time that it's supporting at least one (see Figure 20.2).

Mechanics

This person isn't actually stripping down motor scooters for parts himself. He has hired mechanics to do so.

So there it is! If you want to go into the parts business, buy used products and strip them down for their parts. It may be a great ancillary business to selling new parts on eBay, or it may be a business that stands on its own. What's clear is that the parts business seems to be alive, well, and profitable on eBay.

Just like selling accessories, selling parts is a natural extension for many retail businesses selling repairable products. If you sell used products rather than new products, demanufacturing may be your best source for your parts inventory.

Remanufacturing

We're all familiar with fixer-uppers. It's that little two-bedroom house that looks ramshackle and is selling for a dirt-cheap price. With a good contractor or a lot of sweat equity you can fix it up and modernize it so that it will sell at a generous profit above and beyond the cost of the house plus the cost of the rehabilitation. In fact, there's a lot of people doing rehabs, even amateurs.

If you can do it for a house, why can't you do it for a product? Certainly there are many people dealing in used cameras who buy old or defective cameras on eBay or other places, fix them up with used parts, and then sell them on eBay for a profit. These people illustrate clearly that the fixer-upper idea is not exclusive to the housing market.

It will not come as a surprise to you then that Joe's acquaintance mentioned above, in fact, rehabs used Italian motor scooters from the parts that he strips off other used Italian motor scooters. He puts them in fine working condition. Then he sells them on eBay (see Figure 20.2).

Figure 20.2 Moto Bravo, a demanufacturer and remanufacturer. © 2003-2005 Moto Bravo LLC

Remanufacturing clearly falls into the category of making your own special products for your eBay inventory. This is not for everyone, but it's appropriate for a lot of eBay retailers who may not have considered it yet.

Crafts

The sales of crafts falls under this topic. However, since we covered arts and crafts in Chapter 18, we will not rehash it here. Keep in mind, though, that a craftsperson can serve as a small manufacturer for something that you design or that you contract to have designed by a third party.

Summary

It's difficult to bring this chapter to a close because there are so many possibilities and so few ideas covered here. Most eBay retailers will want to steer clear of getting into the manufacturing business. And rightly so. Yet there will always be eBay retailers who see retail opportunities that can only be exploited by making arrangements to have something made or by making it themselves. It's the quest for the unusual product that might be a big seller. And in many cases it may not be so difficult to pull it off. Many small businesses have done it successfully in the past, and it's not something you should think foolhardy to consider.

21

Between Markets

Buying at a wholesale price in one market and selling at a retail price in another market is an age-old strategy. The markets may be the same market at different times, or different markets. One market can be online and the other offline, or vice versa. It's simply the idea that the markets are out of kilter, and you can exploit the difference profitably.

When this is done in the securities markets (e.g., the stock market), it's called *arbitrage*. But arbitrage is easy to perform in the highly regulated securities markets. Arbitrage is more difficult to pull off in the chaotic retail markets. Proceed cautiously. You need a lot of data about the products and the markets to make this work.

Time and Place

If you can buy in one market at one time and sell in the same market at another time, the time span may enable you to make a profit. For instance, you can buy a sailboat in Madison, Wisconsin, in October, hold the sailboat over the winter, sell the sailboat in Wisconsin in April, and your potential for making a profit is considerable. Everyone is sick of their sailboat in October. Everyone wants a sailboat in April. Thus, you can buy at a wholesale price and sell at a retail price.

Naturally, you have to have considerable capital to carry this inventory for six months. This is particularly true of expensive items such as boats. But certainly there are opportunities for less expensive items too (e.g., summer clothes).

Time

The question you might ask is, how is this relevant to eBay? It's relevant in two ways. First, one might buy summer clothes (excess inventory) from a department store in October and sell them on eBay in April. But there's another opportunity too that compresses the time period.

Place

For example, you could buy the sailboat in Wisconsin in October and sell it to someone on Padre Island (summer-like winters) in Texas in November. You would do this by transporting the boat to Padre Island immediately after the purchase.

Could eBay work here? Sure. People on Padre Island use eBay. Thus, eBay, in effect, removes the time factor and substitutes the geographical factor because eBay reaches Padre Island. In addition, eBay eliminates the need for paying the cost of transportation prior to selling the boat.

Yet if the boat is to be sold on eBay, transportation remains a serious cost factor. You want to sell the boat on Padre Island, in effect, by selling it via eBay. If you want to make this work, you'd better answer the transportation question. That is, you'd better include the cost of transportation in the sales price. Here are two ways for you to minimize the transportation costs and include it in the sales price:

- Transport and deliver the sailboat yourself. The cost-effectiveness of this technique will depend on the magnitude of the sale and the amount of profit you get after paying the cost of transportation.

- Ship only to key locations, not to specific buyer addresses. For instance, as part of the sales price you might include shipping the sailboat to Houston or San Antonio, Texas, for the buyer to pick up at a shipping terminal. Big cities are inexpensive shipping destinations, and this strategy would keep your cost of transportation as low as possible.

Thus, because eBay is a national marketplace, it enables you to buy offline in one market inexpensively (i.e., your local market) and sell on eBay for a profit without the long time lag. Needless to say, this is not automatic. You have to research the markets carefully to make sure that you can make a profit at whatever you propose to do. There is not always a significant profit in working between markets like this. But plenty of opportunities exist to warrant your attention.

More than Padre Island

Your market for the sailboat in November would be broader on eBay than just Padre Island in Texas, of course. It would include all the costal states from Florida to Texas, as well as Southern California. Consequently, the size of this market is more than just local. It includes about 25 percent of the entire US market.

What types of products might you investigate? Boats, RVs, ATVs, cars (e.g., convertibles), motorcycles, bicycles, sports equipment, camping equipment, hunting equipment, and anything else seasonal.

Political Boundaries

This idea doesn't just work between locations in the US market. It also works across political boundaries. Because of restrictions on trade and for other industry reasons, there may be sizable price differences between one product in one country and the same product in another country. Thus, by buying in one country and moving the product across borders to sell in another country, you may be able to realize a greater profit than selling the product in the United States.

For instance, professional books and trade books tend to be expensive in many European countries and elsewhere. Yet in the United States they are relatively cheap. Consequently, it makes sense to acquire such books used at a low price (or even new books at a wholesale price) and sell them on eBay in foreign countries to foreign buyers at a higher price. Anyone who has sold books on eBay US will tell you that they have a large foreign clientele.

Make no mistake: This does not work just for books. It works for a great variety of products. American products are popular abroad. Read Chapter 25 for more on foreign markets. Read *eBay Global the Smart Way* for a thorough coverage of global commerce (import-export) and eBay.

Also read about gray market merchandise in Chapter 24. Selling gray market merchandise is a risky endeavor that can get you into trouble with your customers.

Between Places Online

Can you buy in another online marketplace and then sell on eBay for a profit? You bet! We have found plenty of products for sale on Froogle at discount prices that we could turn around and sell on eBay for a profit. That's just one example. There are plenty of other online marketplaces. Certainly you're also going to find some products cheaper on eBay than on other online marketplaces, and that gives you the opportunity to do just the opposite. Buy on eBay and sell on other online marketplaces where you can sell for a higher price.

One Example

One specific case that's worth mentioning is that eBay has never quite figured out how to do local auctions. But if eBay hasn't learned to run local marketplaces, certainly Craig's List has. Craig's List, without elaborating on how it works, is an excellent local marketplace. Craig's List now operates in over 100 cities both in the United States and abroad. If you can buy something cheap on eBay, it may be profitable to sell it on Craig's List.

Vice Versa

It can work the other way around too. For instance, if you can buy a sailboat on Craig's List in Madison in October and sell it on eBay in November, there's likely some profit potential.

Not Always eBay

The selling scheme doesn't always have to include eBay. How about buying the sailboat on Craig's List in Madison (October) and selling it on Craig's List in San Antonio (November)?

Summary

The idea of buying in one market and selling in another is one eBay sellers have used from the beginning. The challenge is not to do it just once or only occasionally. The challenge is to make a business out of it. In most cases it requires a lot of research, a sound strategy, and some getting set up well in order to make it work. It's another way to get inventory for your eBay retail business.

eBay

eBay itself as a source of inventory? Who knew? Is this one of those touted eBay "secrets"? Well, maybe. eBay retailers have been buying on eBay and then selling on eBay for a profit going back to the very beginning. But this way is just one technique to acquire inventory using eBay. There are others, and this chapter covers a few.

eBay is convenient. You just sit in front of your computer to work. Few telephone calls. Little networking. No traveling. It all happens in the digital telecom ether. Nonetheless, most people who seek inventory via eBay do so to supplement other sources, not as the sole source by itself. And that makes sense for many types of products.

Mismanaged Listings

Mismanaged listings on eBay enable you to buy products inexpensively and, in turn, sell them on eBay to make a profit. For instance, a seller who provides a poor photograph (or no photograph) and lists an item with no reserve price is likely to sell for a price below the normal eBay price for such an item. If the sales price is far enough below normal, it creates an opportunity for you to make a meaningful profit by buying and then selling the item.

Another case is where the seller provides no detailed description of an item. For example, suppose the seller lists the item as a Sony camcorder together with a good photograph but doesn't give the model number, any information, or the condition of the item. There is no reserve price. This item is likely to sell for significantly less than it would if substantial information were provided.

So you come along and analyze the photograph to discern the model number and ascertain that the camcorder appears to be in good condition. Or perhaps you contact the seller to get the information you want, and the seller gives it to you without adding it to the eBay auction ad. You then make a lowball bid. It has a good chance of being the winning bid, thus creating an opportunity for you to make a reasonable profit by buying and then selling the item.

Another situation is one where the seller has misspelled the name of the item in the title line. It will, therefore, be alone by itself and will not show up together with identical or similar items in an eBay search. Consequently, perhaps none of the potential eBay buyers will find it. Again, if it has no reserve, it might sell for a low price providing you an opportunity to make a meaningful profit by buying and then selling the item.

One means of saving time in your searches is to use a website that helps you find eBay seller mistakes. Look at the following:

Fat Fingers, *http://www.fatfingers.co.uk*

TypoBid, *http://www.typobid.com,* see Figure 22.1

Pretty slick! Give them a try. The more time you can save, the better this idea works.

The same idea goes for all kinds of eBay listing mistakes of which there are many (e.g., listing in the wrong category). But there is a cost to acquiring inventory this way. It will take your time and energy to find these mismanaged listings, and you will be spending a lot of time in front of your computer screen. Hence, you have to factor that into the cost-effectiveness of acquiring inventory this way.

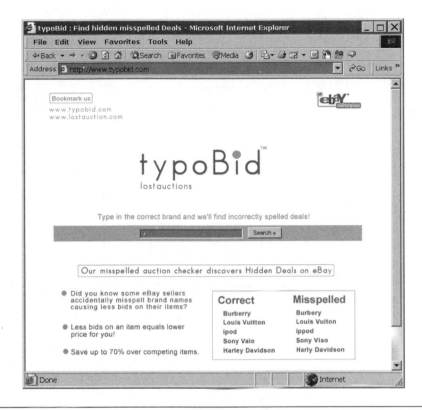

Figure 22.1 TypoBid website. ©2005 TypoBid. All rights reserved.

Picking

Although we have covered picking in Chapter 16, it's worth mentioning here that eBay is a great place to pick. Traditionally and currently, there are a great number of sellers on eBay who are either very eager to get rid of items they don't want or don't know the value of the items they are selling. The result is the opportunity for low sales prices. You may be able to buy items on eBay cheap and sell them elsewhere for a profit, or even sell them on eBay for a profit. This is certainly a popular practice on eBay. Nonetheless, if this technique is compatible with your contemplated eBay retail business, it is worth your serious consideration.

Defective Items

Although this is covered in Chapter 20, it's worth repeating that eBay is terrific source of defective items. The two things you can do with defective items is salvage parts from them or fix them up with salvaged parts to put them in good working order. The parts business is good on eBay, and rehabbed items are worth more than defective items.

Bulk Sales

eBay is a good source, not a great source, of bulk sales. You can expect it to get better over the years. Go to Wholesale Lots by clicking on the Wholesale link on the eBay home page. If you can find bulk sales for your industry, this may be a good source of acquiring inventory in volume at a low price. You will then have to carry such inventory until you can sell it on eBay, one item at a time, to retail customers.

Figure 22.2 eBay Wholesale Lots. ©1995-2005 eBay Inc. All rights reserved.

Also, try the new eBay Reseller Marketplace (*http://reseller.ebay.com*) designed for bulk sales (available only to PowerSellers).

Closeouts

Although we cover closeouts in Chapter 14, some closeout vendors sell closeouts on eBay. Thus, you may be able to buy a pallet or two of closeout items appropriate for your eBay retail business right on eBay. Again, go to Wholesale Lots by clicking on the Wholesale link on the eBay home page. Again try the eBay Reseller Marketplace mentioned above.

From One Market to Another

We have indicated in Chapter 21 that you can sometimes buy in one market low and sell in another market high. Since this is a book about eBay and since you are an eBay retailer, one of those marketplaces is going to be eBay. It's up to you to figure out what the other marketplaces can be. Craig's List, Froogle, Yahoo! Shopping, Amazon, or NexTag are some of the online possibilities, and offline marketplaces might work too. There is significant potential to buy on eBay and sell in another marketplace, or buy in another marketplace and sell on eBay.

A Neat Fit

As an eBay retailer, you will find yourself more and more drawn into other online marketplaces, particularly through datafeed marketing (read Chapter 4) and other cost-effective marketing opportunities. If you take full advantage of online marketing, eBay will become more of a gateway to ecommerce than just a one-market operation for you. Consequently, keeping an eye out for opportunities to buy in one marketplace and sell for a profit in another may fit neatly into your retail operation.

Discover Sources

Want to find sources of inventory? Look at the eBay auctions for your retail niche! There are two opportunities here for you.

First, the obvious. There are wholesalers selling on eBay. You can identify them and get their contact information. What you do after that is a matter of negotiation. If you do talk with a specific wholesaler, almost anything might happen:

- The wholesaler may be willing to sell to you at wholesale prices even though you will be a competitor on eBay.

- The wholesaler might be looking for someone to sell its merchandise on eBay and is only selling itself as a temporary measure.

- The wholesaler may be willing to sell to you at wholesale prices so long as you sell elsewhere online but not on eBay.

- The wholesaler may not be willing to sell to you at wholesale prices.

- Any one of dozens of other possibilities.

If you don't ask, you'll never know what opportunities you may have missed.

The second opportunity is to investigate the retail sellers listing auctions. Where are they getting their products? There may be some good clues right in their auction ads. If they are drop shipping, a purchase of a product might reveal a return address that's a good clue.

You can always contact eBay retailers (as a colleague), preferably by telephone, and ask them about their wholesale sources. It's amazing what people will tell you in a conversation. They may even welcome the competition for dozens of different reasons that make good business sense. There's no harm in trying. The worst that can happen is that they will be uncooperative (uncommunicative). But at least they should be friendly. After all, you are colleagues.

Watch the Marketplace

There are other reasons to look at the eBay auctions in your retail niche:

- You may discover new products.

- You'll stay aware of sales price trends.

- You can observe your competition.

You can spot developing opportunities. The marketplace will give you lots of leads to determine what products will sell and where to find those products. Just being aware will lead to opportunities to acquire inventory.

Summary

As you can see, without beating a dead horse, eBay itself is a potential source of inventory for your eBay retail business. It's smart to keep this in mind at all times because your business and the products you handle will likely change over time. eBay may be a potential source of inventory in the future even if it isn't today.

23

Public Domain

The United States protects the creative works of people and organizations through the copyright laws. These creative works are known as *intellectual property* and include:

- Writings
- Music
- Art

Protection means that the creator has the right to deny use to anyone who desires to use his or her creative work. Anyone who uses copyrighted intellectual property without getting permission violates the law and may be subject to criminal prosecution. In addition, the violator is subject to civil liability; that is, the creator can sue the violator.

Typically, a creator licenses the use of the creative work for a fee to a company that publishes (distributes) it. For instance, an author copyrights a book and gets paid by a publisher. The publisher prints the book and sells (distributes) copies to the public.

Of course, not all intellectual property is published. Nonetheless, a copyright is still in effect. In fact, as soon as a person or company creates a work, a copyright for that creative work is automatically established. If the person or company registers the copyright with the United States Copyright Office, the author gains additional rights under the law. Such additional rights make it easier for a creator to sue a violator and collect damages (money) in a lawsuit.

What Is the Public Domain?

There is a time limit on copyrights. When the time limit runs out, the creative work is said to be in the *public domain*. In other words, the creative work now belongs to the public. Anyone can use it without permission of or payment to the creator.

Time Limits

Copyrights have time limits. Since 1978, the time limit is the life of the creator plus 70 years. Before 1978, the limit was 28 years with provision for a renewal period of another 28 years. However, Congress has adjusted the pre-1978 laws several times to increase the time retroactively in order to accommodate major corporations that have close-to-expiration copyrights in such works as rodent animations. Consequently, the pre-1978 law has become increasingly complex with each Congressional tinkering.

Do individual authors, musicians, and artists have effective lobbying power in Washington? No, but corporations do. The time limits are extended often enough (retroactively) to make sure corporations don't lose their rights to legacy intellectual property. (Your tax dollars in action.)

To figure out what time limit applies to a particular creative work takes a review of the copyright laws. Make no assumptions: the public domain ain't what it used to be.

An Opportunity

Using public domain intellectual property provides you with an opportunity to create products (inventory) inexpensively. You don't have to pay the creator (presumably long dead). However, you need to look at a public domain creative work as just raw material, not as a finished product. You will undoubtedly have to do something with it to turn it into a product that you can sell.

For instance, you can get the text to *Moby Dick*, written by Herman Melville in 1851, free at the Gutenberg Project (*http://www.gutenberg.org*) in electronic form. It's in the public domain. To make it an attractive and useful product, however, you will have to turn the electronic text into an appealing ebook or printed book. Either will require an investment. It takes a competent digital worker to make an attractive ebook, and typesetting and printing a book isn't cheap.

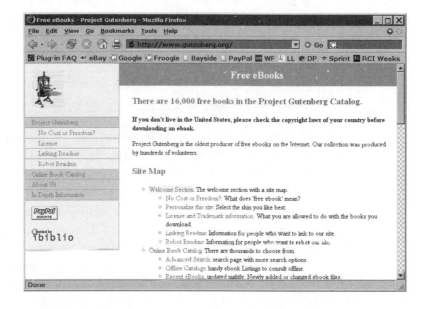

Figure 23.1 Gutenberg Project website. © 2003-2005 Project Gutenberg Literary Archive Foundation. All Rights Reserved.

An Example

In 1997, Alfred A. Knopf, a New York publisher, published *Eyes of the Nation: A Visual History of the United States*, by Vincent Virga and the Curators of the Library of Congress, with historical commentary by Alan Brinkley (ISBN 0-679-44330-4). This is a stunningly appealing book, full of wonderful public domain images from the Library of Congress. Let's analyze it from the point of view of the use of public domain images.

The Images The images are all public domain from the archives of the Library of Congress and are themselves not copyrightable.

The Prints of the Images The prints of the images on the pages of the book are presumably copyrighted. Making a printing plate starts with a photograph. Photographing the images from the archives is a creative process making the photographs protected by the copyright laws.

The Book The book consists of new text (copyrightable) and printed images resulting from new photographs of the public domain images (copyrightable). Consequently, the book is entirely copyrighted.

The question arises: What can you use from this book without violating the copyright laws? The answer is, nothing. For example, if you were to use a high-resolution scanner to scan one of the high-quality images printed in the book, you would not be able to use such an image without the permission of the publisher even though it's a public domain image. It's actually a copyrightable copy of the public domain image.

But hold on. This story gets more interesting. ArtLook, Inc., a company in Virginia, made a multimedia CD using the content of the book. On the CD are all the public domain images in digital form. This makes them quite easy to use. Indeed, you could easily digitally copy one of the digital images on the CD and use it to print a beautiful, full-color copy of the image. Unfortunately, these images are presumably copyrightable. They are photographs of the images from the archives and are copyrightable creative works themselves.

What Do You Do?

Let's say you want to use one of these images to make an attractive poster to sell to college students via eBay. What do you do? You could scan the image in the book, but you would have to get permission of the publisher to use the image. The book publisher would likely charge a licensing fee. You could use the digital image on the CD, but the CD publisher would likely charge a licensing fee.

That leaves you to go to the Library of Congress in Washington, DC, and arrange to make your own copy (photograph) of the public domain image. In fact, the Library may already have made a high-quality copy of the image that you can buy for a nominal amount and use. (While in Washington, you might do well to browse through the hundreds of thousands of other images the Library of Congress has archived.)

Fortunately, you don't even have to go to Washington. Go to the Library of Congress website (*http://www.loc.gov*) to see what's available. Check the Prints & Photographs Reading Room (*http://www.loc.gov/rr/print/catalog.html*). See Figure 23.2 for an example of what you might find and Figure 23.4 for a product created therefrom.

Figure 23.2 Photograph of General Grant of Civil War fame (and later President) from the Library of Congress. This is from the Brady-Handy collection.

Figure 23.3 Photograph of General Grant with five minutes work in Adobe Photoshop CS2.

Is there a new product here somewhere? Well, if you don't think a T-shirt with General Grant on the back will sell, there are plenty more images where this one came from available from the public domain in the Library of Congress and elsewhere.

Be Careful

Your conclusion from reading this section should be that you need to be careful when using public domain intellectual property. For instance, to use images, you may have to go to the originals and make your own reproductions. Each type of intellectual property (each medium) has its own considerations in regard to the copyright laws. We have used images in this chapter simply as one example. You will need to pay attention to the entire copyright law.

Nolo Press (*http://nolo.com*) publishes legal guides for lay people. You can get its latest guide on the copyright laws and should find it readable.

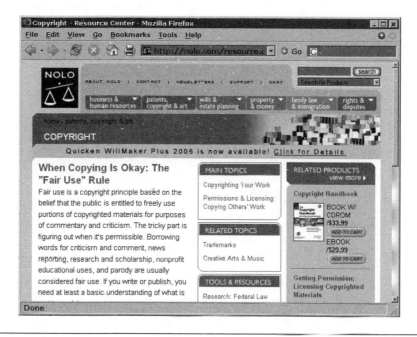

Figure 23.4 Nolo Press copyright webpage.

Summary

The public domain offers you opportunities to acquire products—at no cost—for your inventory of intellectual property. If that's what you sell, this might prove a profitable source for you. Keep in mind, however, that intellectual property from the public domain is seldom in saleable form. You will need to create something new using it. Therein lies the true cost of this inventory.

24

Inventory Scams

Starting an eBay retail business is a great opportunity for many people and has a huge amount of potential for profits and financial self-sufficiency. Nonetheless, it's not a get-rich-quick scheme. Like any small business, it takes a lot of hard work, persistence, sound information, common sense, and even luck to be successful. Therefore, anyone who tells you otherwise is a prima facie scammer. And there's no shortage of them lurking around in eBay auctions and other places online, advertising in business magazines, and making presentations in multi-city tours. Watch out!

You've heard it said: If it's too good to be true, it undoubtedly is. Most of the scammers use promises that are too good to be true to get you to buy information, products (inventory), or services that you are better off without. It is to this fraud that this chapter is devoted. I guess you could say this is a "source" of inventory to avoid.

Information and Inventory

There is plenty of information available on eBay and on the Web about how to find wholesale inventory to sell at a profit. Most of it is worthless.

It is difficult to find suppliers that will sell to small businesses. It is particularly hard to find suppliers that will drop ship. In addition, to keep a list updated takes an ongoing effort. This translates into the fact that it's expensive to provide this information. Consequently, cheap lists of inventory sources are invariably worthless.

Typical information sources are often copies of a list of suppliers someone found on the Web five years ago seeking to make a quick buck selling information. Unfortunately, legitimate wholesalers aren't on the Web seeking to get small retailers as customers. They never were.

This information, where legitimate and available, is usually a service for a modest (but not cheap) monthly fee. But you can't go by price alone because many scammers know people equate price with value. They simply put a high price on their worthless information.

Then, too, there are suppliers that provide inventory to wannabe retailers at high wholesale prices, which in some cases exceed retail prices. Drop shipping is a common part of the offering. These suppliers are often middlemen (retailers, jobbers, brokers, or just plain scam artists) not offering normal wholesale prices. Often the merchandise is substandard and not easily saleable. This scam is a holdover from the get-rich-with-mail-order days.

Signs of a Scam

What are the signs that information or inventory is probably worthless?

- Promises that you will get rich
- Claims that you can make $5,000 a week in your spare time (or fill in another amount)
- Copy writing that is long and enticing but makes claims that are not substantiated
- Multiple extra information products or other products are included
- No contact information (person, company, address, telephone number, email address)
- Claims of making presentations in major cities around the country

- Promises to reveal eBay "secrets" or reveal what <u>PowerSellers</u> don't want you to know (fill in the blank)
- Promises to tell you what PowerSellers are doing
- Very high price (e.g., $4,000)
- Very low price (e.g., $4)
- Account setup fee is required

Each of these by itself is not necessarily a sign of worthlessness. But a few taken together makes a stronger case.

At Websites

If you're looking for information at websites, look for the About Us or Contact Us links (or something similar). That should give you all the contact information you need—if the links exist on the website. If not, move on.

Secrets in Books

There are no secrets about how to find inventory or operate an eBay retail business. Some authors cover some things and other authors cover other things. There is usually a huge overlap. And what's unique to each author is likely covered by a third author. Every time we read the promos about the "secrets" an author claims to reveal, the secrets turn out to be mostly mundane stuff that almost everybody knows. Even major publishers have resorted to this type of shoddy promotion, presumably to mask books that have little unique character.

Ask

What are some things you can ask for, if you can find a place to ask?

- Founder of service
- Location of service
- The history of the service
- Number of employees
- Relationship to eBay (e.g., Certified eBay Developer, etc.)
- Referrals (with contact information)

- Help desk or other support
- Sample wholesale prices for specific products
- Free trial (before payment, not refund based on guarantee)

Following the Lead of PowerSellers

Some eBay books and services advocate that if you just follow the lead of ostensibly successful eBay sellers (i.e., PowerSellers), you will be successful. And they will be happy to help you for a price. That is, do what PowerSellers are doing, and you will get rich quick. Unfortunately, this idea contains some fallacies.

PowerSellers

PowerSellers by definition must sell at least $1,000 of goods a month to qualify for this eBay designation. Assume a 15 percent net profit. That's only $150 a month profit, hardly enough to live on. In other words, eBay obviously intends the PowerSeller designation for active non-commercial sellers and part-time retail sellers as well as full-time retail sellers. Indeed, just to be a PowerSeller doesn't mean much in the ecommerce world.

Levels

There are different categories for the PowerSeller designation requiring different levels of monthly sales:

Bronze	$1,000
Silver	$3,000
Gold	$10,000
Platinum	$25,000
Titanium	$150,000

In fact, you might be quite interested in what a Titanium PowerSeller is doing while at the same time have little interest in what a Bronze PowerSeller is doing.

Designation Voluntary

Not all eligible eBay retailers are PowerSellers. The designation is voluntary and requires accepting an invitation. The designation is not automatically bestowed. Some successful eBay retailers do not bother to become PowerSellers because the benefits of the eBay PowerSeller program are not compelling to them.

PESA

The Professional eBay Sellers Alliance (PESA – *http://www.gopesa.org* – see Figure 24.1) is an independent organization of eBay retailers. To join, you must sell $25,000 of goods a month on eBay. To be a member of this organization is much more meaningful vis-a-vis financial success than just to be a PowerSeller. Yet assuming a 15 percent net profit, that's $3,750 a month ($45,000 a year), not an amount that will enable you to get rich quickly.

Figure 24.1 PESA website. ©2005 Professional eBay Sellers Alliance

Profit

The assumption in the above examples is that you will achieve a 15 percent net profit before paying yourself. That's just an arbitrary percentage we pulled out of the air. In fact, for many products such a net profit may not be possible. And there are many eBay businesses that make more than 15 percent.

No Guarantee of Success

What works for someone who is successful won't necessarily work for you. The merchandise you choose to sell is based on personal criteria as well as market criteria. It might be a big mistake to go chasing after other seemingly successful eBay sellers (e.g., PowerSellers) and trying to imitate or duplicate their successes.

Indeed, just identifying which sellers are successful (and which are not) is difficult to do. For instance, how do you determine another eBay retailer's net profit? And success itself—once identified—has many hidden factors other than net profit.

eBay is not a get-rich-quick scheme that follows some formula established by others. Being successful on eBay requires hard work and an intelligent approach to chosing your products and your market niches. Watching what PowerSellers or others are doing probably won't hurt, but that by itself is not a magic formula for success.

Moral

The moral of this story is that what PowerSellers do does not necessarily point the way to eBay success. Many PowerSellers are unsuccessful or marginal eBay retailers. Although some PowerSellers do quite well financially, it's clear that being a PowerSeller is not definitive by itself without additional information in regard to sales and profits.

Please Note

The purpose of this section is obviously not to belittle PowerSellers who are undoubtedly a fine group of people, many of whom are quite successful on eBay.

It's likely that anyone who uses the alleged wisdom of PowerSellers indiscriminately to promote the sale of inventory services or information is using an eBay buzz word for promotion purposes without regard to reality. In other words, they're out to get your money, not to enlighten you. There is no one-size-fits-all scheme to becoming successful on eBay.

Multilevel Marketing

Multilevel marketing (MLM) is a business that works—for very few people. If you're interested in MLM, we suggest you buy several credible books on it from a bookstore, read them, find out what you have to do to be successful, and then decide whether MLM is for you. Most people will decide it's not the career route they wish to take.

It's intensely hard work for those who are successful and requires deep leadership skills. Hint: Getting in on the ground floor has nothing to do with success. For example, many people who have been very successful with Amway (a successful MLM company) joined after the company had already been in business for thirty years.

You need to investigate this before you seriously consider an MLM offering. That's the only way you will be able to make an objective decision.

Most MLM schemes are doomed to failure. There are just enough that do achieve some success to generate eternal hope that the next MLM scheme—the one you are considering—will be a jackpot. But you have two strikes against you going in. First, few people have what it takes to be successful even in a successful MLM scheme. Second, there are few successful MLM schemes.

If you want to be an eBay retailer, save yourself a huge amount of wasted time by staying away from MLM schemes related to eBay retailing. Just say no. Hey, we might not be talking about fraud here, although some MLM schemes are fraudulent, but the effect is the same. For the money you make, if any, before you get out, you will squander more time (and perhaps money) than you thought possible.

Visit the MLM Watch website (*http://www.mlmwatch.org* – see Figure 24.2) for skeptical information on MLM schemes. It might even have information about the specific MLM offering you are considering.

Web Hosting Services

Providing Web hosting services is a very competitive business. The result is that you can find a host Internet service provider (ISP) that enables you to build a website for your eBay retail business that is easy to use, fully functional, ecommerce friendly, and inexpensive. Monthly website hosting costs are as little as $5 and include more features than you are ever likely to use. So beware of any inventory service that purports to provide you with a website for your business in addition to providing inventory, usually for a considerable fee.

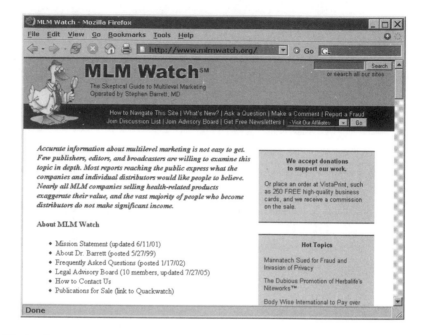

Figure 24.2 MLM Watch website.

It's usually an offer like this, "We provide the inventory and your website, and all you do is collect the checks." Yah, right! Don't waste your money.

Beware the Gray

Beware of gray market merchandise when buying inventory abroad (or even in the US). Name-brand merchandise is often sold cheaper abroad than in the US. You can buy it abroad and sell it domestically at a profit. In doing so, however, you are creating a *gray market*. How's that?

Gray market merchandise may have slightly different features. The owner's manual may not be in English. The product will not be eligible for any US rebate programs. The foreign version of the product may not comply with certain governmental regulations in the US. And the manufacturer will not honor the warranty in the US.

Software

Gray market software is usually not registerable, and owners will not be eligible for the upgrade pricing on future versions of the software. And by the way, selling software designated for the academic community (it's less expensive) to buyers who are not teachers or students is a gray market activity too.

Go to the Alliance for Gray Market and Counterfeit Abatement (AGMA) website (*http://agmaglobal.org*) for more information on the gray market. The AGMA is supported by such companies as Cisco Systems, Hewlett-Packard, and Seagate.

As you can understand, gray market merchandise is likely to get you into trouble with your customers. If you sell gray market merchandise, you are bound to get negative feedback.

Once you have made the decision not to sell gray market merchandise (a good decision), you need to be sure that suppliers abroad—and in the United States, too—don't sell you gray market merchandise. Selling gray market merchandise to unwary eBay retailers is one of the biggest ongoing scams around.

Gray?

A product for which warranties are typically non-existent or of little value, for which no rebate programs exist, for which there's no owner's manual, and for which governmental regulations are not relevant, does not fit the concept of the gray market. For instance, a digital camera made in Japan and bought abroad is a gray market product if sold in the US. But an ordinary frying pan made in France and bought abroad is not necessarily considered a gray market product if sold in the US.

Counterfeits

Counterfeits can be merchandise as well as money. Usually the type of merchandise counterfeited is small, simple, easy-to-copy, and valuable. A Rolex watch is a good example. Many manufacturers make watches that look like a Rolex, so it's not difficult to make one that copies a Rolex almost exactly in detail—that is, except for the jewels, gold, and inner workings.

Well, we all know that phony jewels and gold look as good—and often better than—the real thing. But who opens a Rolex to look inside? And what would they look for? The fact is that a $15 quartz crystal watch can tell time accurate to a few seconds a year. Consequently, it's neither difficult nor expensive to give a phony Rolex the inner workings to tell time superbly. The problem is that a $3,000 Rolex can be duplicated in appearence for the uninitiated (most of us) for less than $25.

How do you tell the difference? Hey, we don't know. We don't have a clue. The point is that if you're selling Rolexes to people, you had better be able to spot a counterfeit, or you're going to get yourself in a lot of hot water.

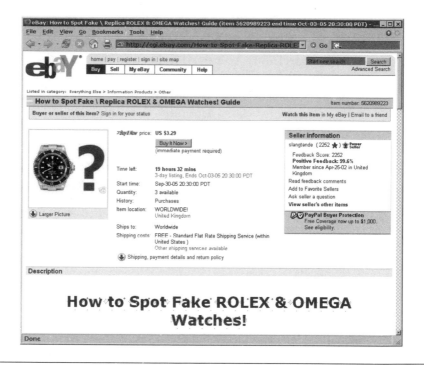

Figure 24.3 Someone selling on eBay wants to make you better informed in regard to fake Rolexes. ©1995-2005 eBay Inc. All Rights Reserved.

Summary

To do justice to this topic, we would have to devote an entire book to it. People desiring to become eBay retailers, and even people who are seasoned eBay retailers, will get taken by inventory scams. That's a certainty. Only by learning about a variety of inventory scams, researching your potential sources of inventory carefully, and never committing to large orders until a source is proven, will you avoid this pitfall on your way to eBay retailing success.

IV

Special Opportunities

25

Foreign Goods

eBay is a terrific place to sell imports. If you buy your inventory properly, imports tend to be exotic, unique, and often comparatively inexpensive products that are easy to sell. The question is, where do you get such products? Read *eBay Global the Smart Way* for a comprehensive treatment of this particular topic and the means of acquiring inventory. Suffice to say here that you can visit the foreign eBays, of which there are now 30. There you can find interesting products being sold. Through the seller, you may be able to arrange a steady supply of such products at wholesale prices. Obviously, this approach will take a lot of research and a lot of Web surfing.

Another way is to simply travel abroad and go on a shopping spree. While you're abroad, trace down the wholesalers for the products that you want to sell and make arrangements to buy at wholesale and import.

Importing in trivial quantities is easy to do, and you can use the normal means of shipment such as the Postal Service, UPS, and FedEx. For larger quantities, bulk air shipments may be too expensive. You may want to ship via an ocean vessel instead. And to import large quantities, you will need to pay a customs broker or a freight forwarder to get the goods through customs. Although this sounds like a lot of trouble to go to, it's easier than you think.

In fact, it has never been easier to go into the import-export business than today. By using eBay in foreign countries, you can avoid the travel expense that you'd otherwise almost certainly have getting into the import business. And with an eBay US retail business, the market for such exotic goods, and even practical goods, is much larger than operating an import-export shop in your community. This, indeed, is a fabulous opportunity and is one that seems to be underutilized on eBay in the US.

International Trade Shows

There are international trade shows that appear in the US occasionally. These are industry trade shows that move around from country to country just as national trade shows move around from city to city within the US. There are also trade shows held in the US specifically to enable foreign manufacturers and wholesalers to acquire retailers and wholesalers in the US. Consequently, you have two resources for getting acquainted with foreign products and making the requisite contacts to buy inventory and import it. Although these events tend to take place on the East Coast or the West Coast, they occasionally take place in inland cities, particularly inland cities with international airports. Read Chapter 9 in regard to this idea for further information on trade shows in general.

World Trade Centers

Just like there are trade marts in many major cities as covered in Chapter 9, there are also World Trade Centers. Check the World Trade Centers Association website (*http://wtca.org*). Find out if there is a World Trade Center in your city or a nearby city. This is like a trade mart for foreign manufacturers and wholesalers and may prove to be an excellent source of products to import and sell on eBay. In fact, the manufacturers and wholesalers may even have gone through the importing process for you and have such goods available for your purchase in US warehouses.

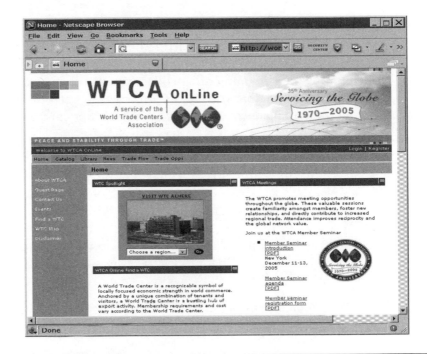

Figure 25.1 World Trade Centers Association website.

Foreign Closeouts

As you can imagine, once you get plugged into the import industry, you will start to become aware through industry notices or otherwise that there are foreign closeouts comparable to closeouts in the US.

Foreign closeouts can be an excellent low-cost means of acquiring inventory that you can sell for a profit on eBay. You would probably be surprised at how many eBay retailers have taken advantage of this particular source of high-quality goods to be sold.

Case Study

Joe talked with an eBay retailer who bought 3,000 heart rate monitors (for athletes) in Taiwan in a closeout and then imported them. Joe asked him if that wasn't a huge number of monitors. He said that it was but that if he didn't buy the entire closeout, some other eBay retailer would buy the remainder. He didn't want the competition on eBay.

Manufacturing Abroad

If you have a need to manufacture products, we will first advise you to find a domestic manufacturer. It's very embarrassing to have a foreign manufacturer manufacture goods for you only to find that you could have them manufactured in the United States at a lower cost. Foreign manufacturing does not always offer the lowest cost or highest quality.

Nonetheless, foreign manufacturing can be an excellent source of inventory for goods that you need to have manufactured. Unfortunately, it's more difficult to arrange manufacturing with foreign companies than it is with domestic ones. But with today's inexpensive communication and the ability to find foreign manufacturers on the Web, it may be less trouble than you might think. In addition, when you visit a foreign country, it provides you with an excellent opportunity to go directly to manufacturers, visit their factories, and negotiate a supply of inventory on the spot.

Do Your Homework

Because your legal recourse may be limited in foreign countries, it pays to do your homework and check up on potential manufacturers. Jeremy has a friend who speaks fluent Chinese and negotiated with a Chinese manufacturer to produce a special kind of retro-styled bicycle.

After the first run of several thousand bikes was complete, Jeremy's friend was horrified to discover that the manufacturer had used an inferior grade of steel, and the bikes couldn't be ridden without bending and breaking. The manufacturer had required a significant deposit in order to proceed with the manufacturing run, and under Chinese law it would be nearly impossible to get the deposit back. Luckily, he was able to convince the manufacturer to use a higher grade of steel and re-do the run with the promise of future business.

Surprisingly, it has been our experience that foreign manufacturing is possible to do even for small quantities of certain goods. There are small factories throughout Asia, for example, that would be happy to manufacture your products in a short production run at a low cost.

Alibaba

Alibaba (*http://alibaba.com*) is an online directory of Chinese manufacturers. The manufacturers have been screened at two levels. The first level is to determine on paper whether they are legitimate or not. The second level is an actual visit to their factory to inspect the quality of their manufacturing operation. Consequently, the directory makes it very practical for you to get in direct touch with Chinese manufacturers to manufacture your products. The old way of doing this was to do it through an intermediary, often an expensive proposition, particularly for small runs of products. In fact, the old way is pretty much still in effect. However, Alibaba creates a new opportunity for you to deal direct and save money.

Figure 25.2 The Alibaba website. ©1999-2005 Alibaba.com Corporation and its licensors. All rights reserved.

Although this seems like a terrific opportunity—and it is—it's not one to be taken lightly. You are well advised to research how to do business in China thoroughly before you undertake to contact any factory in the Alibaba directory. This is no small undertaking. But with the resources of the Web and the proliferation of import-export books, it's certainly possible to learn quickly. Again, we recommend *eBay Global the Smart Way* as a starting point for you.

Incidently, Alibaba was founded by the same person—Jack Ma—who founded the Chinese online marketplace Taobao (*http://www.taobao.com*), which competes directly with eBay in China. Will you find Alibaba exhibiting at the annual eBay conference? Probably not. In 2005, it was not in the conference but at a hotel next door.

Figure 25.3 The Taobao website. ©2003-2005 TAOBAO.COM

Global Sources

Global Sources (*http://www.globalsources.com*) is another online directory. This one provides you direct access to suppliers in Hong Kong, mainland China, and Taiwan. There is a gold mine of possibilities here.

The Roadblock

Okay, so there's a big roadblock between you and cashing in on the ideas in this chapter: it's language. Dealing with foreign manufacturers, wholesalers, and retailers can provide you profitable sales in the United States, but language can be a barrier.

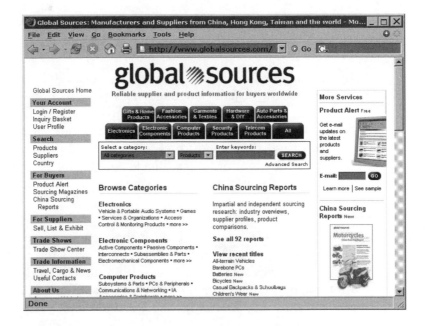

Figure 25.4 The Global Sources website. ©2005 Trade Media Holdings Ltd. ©2005 Trade Media Ltd. All rights reserved.

There are some ways to get around the roadblock:

- Use a language dictionary (e.g., English-Spanish)
- Hire a translator for writing (e.g., a student part-time)
- Hire a translator for speaking (e.g., someone fluent)
- Use a digital translator on the Web

This last idea doesn't work well for commercial activities, but it's something you should try. It's easy. Go to one of the following:

BabelFish Translation, *http://babelfish.altavista.com*

Google, *http://www.google.com/language_tools?hl=en*

Although sources of language translation may seem awkward or too expensive, the import business can become so profitable that it will be worthwhile going out of your way to handle the language difficulties.

Keep in mind also that English is spoken as a primary language by 375 million people. It is spoken as a second language by another 375 million people. And it is spoken as a foreign language by an additional 750 million people. Consequently, there are a total of 1.5 billion people worldwide who speak English.

In addition to these impressive numbers, it is well known that English has become the de facto language of business worldwide. Therefore, it is likely in many situations in the import business, language will not be a roadblock for you. You may have a hard time understanding other people's English through thick accents and broken vocabulary, but that's a distraction, not a roadblock. And thank your lucky stars that you live in a country whose language is used worldwide for business.

The Future

You think you have it tough with these ecommerce problems from abroad? Language. Customs. Shipping. What's the alternative? Well, a lot of factories abroad are now selling directly to the public via the Internet, bypassing normal retail channels offline or online. Think of the problems they are facing—and overcoming!

For instance, look at Panama Hats Direct (*http://panamahatsdirect.com*), an English-language Web outlet for custom-made Panama hats straight from the factory in Montecristi, Ecuador. The hats range in price from $120 to $290. Contrast that with the Panama Hat Company of the Pacific (*http://brentblack.com*), a Hawaiian online retailer that also sells custom-made Panama hats also made in Montecristi. Its prices range from $425 to $825 for the same top quality. Which brings up an interesting question: Will factory outlets online compete with the retail sales infrastructure online? Hey, it's happening already.

This trend should put some mission in your madness. If you cannot provide superb customer service and perhaps some other value-added in your eBay retail business, why wouldn't you be replaced by online factory outlets? In other words, if you don't take on the extra problems of importing appropriate products for inclusion in your retail sales, you will eventually find yourself competing with suppliers that will have been forced into marketing and selling on their own. These are sellers that might have provided you with a wealth of profitable inventory.

Take a close look at Panama Hat Company of the Pacific. It provides tremendous value-added just by the prolific information it provides on its website about Panama hats. In addition, it romanticizes the hats to the point where you can hardly bear to be without one.

Not Owned by the Factory

In the above example, the Web outlet is not owned by the factory because there is no single factory. There are lots of hat factories in Montecristi, many so small that they may not even be considered factories. They're more like workshops. The marketing organization Panama Hats Direct is a small company in Ecuador owned and operated by an American and his Ecuadorian wife.

In many small towns and villages abroad where attractive products are made in small-scale production, a typical business might be a marketing cooperative or a small local marketing company. The local cooperative or company is, in effect, a wholesale distributor which sell its products directly to the global public via the Web.

Manufacturers that sell directly to the public regardless may also be good sources of inventory for you. Many will welcome another means of distribution.

Summary

Getting inventory abroad is easier than you may think. Sure, there are the extra hoops to jump through, such as customs clearance and finding the most inexpensive shipping. But it's never been easier to find products abroad and make arrangements to acquire them for your inventory. Today, with the World Trade Centers, you never have to leave the States; and with the Web, you never have to leave your computer.

People look for unique and useful products, even on eBay. Your imports can bring some foreign spice to eBay US and enlarge your inventory and profits while offering customers choices they never had before.

26

Pawnshops

A pawnshop is a place where people go when they need money. They borrow money using a personal asset (e.g., electric guitar) as collateral. If they don't pay off the loan (and redeem the asset) within the agreed period, the pawnshop owner (pawnbroker) has the right to sell the asset. Pawnbrokers never make such loans unless secured by assets they know they can sell because most loans are not paid off. Consequently, in a pawnshop, you will always find plenty of things for sale, mostly used things.

There is no shortage of pawnshops. If there's not one in your town, there's probably one in a nearby town.

Local Shops

You probably don't need this book to tell you that local pawnshops might be a good source of inventory to sell on eBay. But bear with us. There's more in this chapter.

Not an Ongoing Source

The problem with your local pawnshop is that although it might be a source of inventory for you to sell on eBay, it is probably not an ongoing source of inventory. This is particularly true if you sell into a specialized niche. A local pawnshop is a more valuable source for an eBay retailer that sells anything he or she can get his or her hands on at a low price.

So Many, So Near

There are a lot of pawnshops. There might be more near you than you would think. If you can line up four or five within a 20-mile radius, you may have discovered a signficant source of inventory that will keep your sales humming.

Global Pawn

Global Pawn (*http://www.globalpawn.com*) is a nationwide and worldwide network of pawnbrokers. How does Global Pawn get thousands of pawnshops online with their inventory? Global Pawn first integrated itself into the pawnshop management software available to pawnshops. There are about seven major pawnshop software vendors. By integrating itself into such software, Global Pawn can request and receive a datafeed from every pawnshop nationally or internationally that uses the software. Since there are thousands of pawnshops using such software, Global Pawn is able to feed all the inventory of such pawnshops into its database. It claims to have 11,000,000 items for sale on its website.

It's beyond the scope of this book to teach you how to use Global Pawn, but it's easy to use and has a catalog similar to other online catalogs. Give it a try!

Unfortunately, as this book goes to press, Global Pawn is in the process of ironing out the bugs and shortcomings in its website and database. If you find that it isn't very usable or valuable to you when you first access it, stay tuned for further developments. Give it a try occasionally until all its intended features operate smoothly. It appears to be a potentially terrific and fruitful source of inventory.

The idea here, of course, is to buy low on Global Pawn, and sell high on eBay. Not all the prices on Global Pawn are going to be lower than the comparable prices on eBay for any particular product, and indeed some might even sell for higher prices. Nonetheless, Global Pawn gives you a terrific place to shop for low-cost products.

How do you tell whether a product is going to sell for a higher price on eBay? Simply go to eBay's archive of completed items (Completed Listings) and see what similar or identical items have been selling for for the last four or five weeks. That will give you a pretty good idea of whether or not you can make a profit by buying on Global Pawn and selling on eBay.

Figure 26.1 The Global Pawn website. ©2002-2004 GlobalPawn.com.

Summary

Individual pawnshops by themselves may not be a reliable source of items. But hook up thousands to the Web and catalog their inventory, and now you've got something. GlobalPawn is a website you'll want to learn to use.

27

Finding Market Opportunities

Chapter 1 puts forth basic advice on finding products that you can sell profitably on eBay. It's a basic approach with which many people will feel comfortable. If you have no idea of what you want to sell on eBay even after reading Chapter 1, however, some of the ideas in this chapter may suit your needs better.

In essence, this chapter is not different from Chapter 1. In fact, it augments Chapter 1. It considers in more detail the market research strategy for finding and testing products. It enables you to better spot opportunities for selling profitably. But market research is never the total answer to successful retailing. You must take what you learn here together with the information provided in Chapter 1 to build a retail operation that will bring the profits you seek.

Market Research

Despite what the get-rich-quick-on-eBay authors would have you believe, market research is work. Market research is essentially doing your homework. And homework is typically not a frivolous or short-lived endeavor.

There are two roles for research in your quest to find products. The first is using statistics to identify opportunities to sell (i.e., to identify products that may sell well). You can even extend this to identifying niches where the potential demand is greater than the current sales. The second is to test the market once you have determined that a product might be right for your eBay retail business.

In this book, we are concerned not with maximizing sales (read *Building Your eBay Traffic the Smart Way* for that) but rather with picking products to include in inventory that have a high profit.

Data

eBay keeps the records of all its transactions. It has huge databases. Corporations use a technique called *data mining* to glean general information (e.g., trends) out of their databases. Wouldn't it be great if you could do that with eBay's data? Actually you can, indirectly.

eBay Web Services

eBay offers Web services to qualified vendors. This means that eBay sells its data to vendors. More specifically, it means that eBay enables vendors to tap in electronically to eBay databases and glean *general information* in real time.

General information as the term is used here means that one cannot get information on a specific transaction. One can get only statistics. However, you can get statistics from a very small portion of the data.

Andale

For example, the auction management service Andale (*http:// andale.com*) offers research services. One of the services is Andale What's Hot. Here are some of the features of What's Hot:

- Browse any category to see how many hot items there are.
- Find out the top-selling items in each category.
- Determine the level of competition for any item.
- Find out the average number of bids and the high and low bids for any item.
- Use Andale's Hot Rating, which assesses an item's demand.
- Get useful selling statistics on any product.

- Export What's Hot data to your Excel spreadsheet for further analysis.

Wow! All this data at your fingertips. This is the kind of information for which corporations and huge retailers pay millions. And you can get it very inexpensively through an auction management service that acquires it via eBay Web services.

Another Andale service is Andale Research. This service is more focused on pricing and maximizing prices than it is identifying products, but it can be valuable in testing products in the marketplace. It also provides comparisons to other marketplaces such as Froogle, Bizrate, and Shopping.com.

Finally, Andale offers its Sales Analyzer, which will analyze your sales in a test marketing effort.

DeepAnalysis 2

HammerTap (*http://www.hammertap.com*) has a program DeepAnalysis 2, which uses eBay data and provides analysis comparable to Andale's analytical services. This is definitely a tool you will want to evaluate before you commit yourself to a research service. HammerTap also sells auction managemenet software.

Market Research Wizard

This is a free tool for members of the World Wide Brands (*http://www.worldwidebrands.com* – see Figure 27.1) drop shipping directory service. You can give it a free trial at the website. A recent search used the following inputs for a popular model of a quiet-water kayak made by a leading kayak manufacturer:

Input for eBay category: necky kayak

Input for product: Zoar

Input for brand name: Necky

The search yielded the following outputs:

33 searches on eBay in last 30 days

1 for sale on eBay

0 for sale in eBay Stores

5 for sale in Yahoo! Stores

504 pages on Google that include the search words

40 Overture ads for product

0 Google ads

The Wizard analysis indicated a 56 percent probability of selling this product successfully (considered *good* probability) and showed the current pricing on eBay auctions. It also indicated available drop shipping suppliers and wholesale suppliers. It even identified competitors. This isn't a comprehensive survey of its features, but you can see that it's a useful research tool.

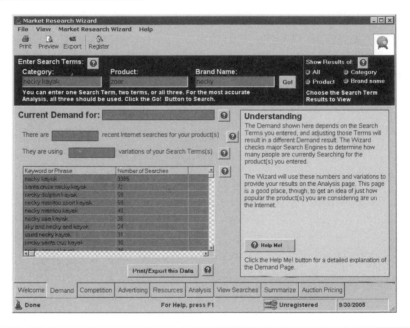

Figure 27.1 Market Research Wizard.

Terapeak

Another research service is Terapeak (*http://www.terapeak.com*). Unlike Andale and HammerTap, Terapeak does not offer auction management software. It's strictly a marketplace research service and uses eBay data. It will help you:

- Value your products
- Save time with accurate searches
- Understand your competition
- Find new products to sell
- Identify highest volume categories
- Study growth trends
- Filter by success rate

And you can export your data for further analysis (e.g., in Excel). Don't commit to research software without evaluating this service too.

Getting Started

One way to get started with Terapeak is to simply drill down into an eBay category. When you drill down to the bottom (i.e., the lowest few subcategories), you get some useful information. For instance, suppose you want to get data on point and shoot digital cameras. You start with the Cameras & Photo category and drill down to Point & Shoot:

Cameras & Photo > Digital Cameras > Point & Shoot

The next seven subcategories sort the point and shoot cameras by the megapixel size of their photo sensors (e.g., 5-MP digital point and shoot cameras). This is the bottom of the category tree, and Terapeak provides you with data for this level (see Figure 27.2).

In the donut chart, it compares the market shares of the subcategories. Thus, we learn the following:

Camera MPs	Market Share (percent)
0 > 1.9	2
2.0 > 2.9	3
3.0 > 3.91	2
4.0 > 4.9	21
5.0 > 5.9	42
6.0 > 6.9	4
7.0 +	16

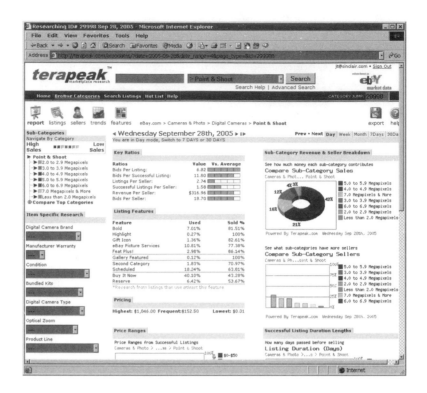

Figure 27.2 Terapeak subcategories (point and shoot), Report page. ©2005
AERS, Inc. All rights reserved.

Looks like the 5-MP subcategory is your most active market. Just
below the donut chart it shows what percentage of sellers are selling in
each category. For instance, a little over 25 percent of the sellers sell in
the 5-MP category, which has a 42 percent market share. About 12
percent of the sellers sell in the 2-MP category, which has a 3 percent
market share. This is interesting and useful information.

It also gives the listing features (e.g., bold type) and shows how often
they were used and what the sales rate was for each.

From there you can pick a category (e.g., 5 to 5.9 MP cameras) and
drill down further (see Figure 27.3) This time the subcategories are
actual name-brand cameras (e.g., Nikon).

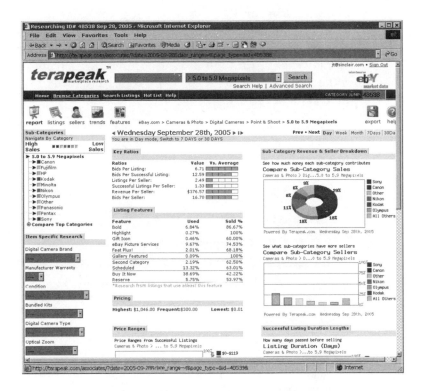

Figure 27.3 Terapeak subcategories (5 to 5.9 MP), Report page. ©2005 AERS, Inc. All rights reserved.

This is just a sample of the information available, and there's more. You can also see a Listings page, a Sellers page, a Trends page, and a Features page, all with loads of useful information. This will help you evaluate products for possible inclusion in your inventory.

Using Keywords

To find individual items, you can search on keywords. For illustration, we searched on "SD400 Canon" camera, a point and shoot digital camera. It returned a report page indicating 5,588 items found for the month of September together with other useful information (see Figure 27.4).

It also returned a Listings page (see Figure 27.5) similar to eBay's Completed Listings page, although somewhat enhanced. You can elect a Day, 7-Days, or 30-Days mode. It gives you the total sales, average price, total listings, total bids, and success rate. It's a cleaner and more useful webpage than eBay's, and you can access each eBay auction listing webpage through it. It also shows the percent of items returned in the category results (e.g., 43 percent were cameras, 26 percent were fitted camera cases, etc.).

And don't forget you get data on Sellers and Trends too. This information will give you a good handle on the current market for individual products and also on market history.

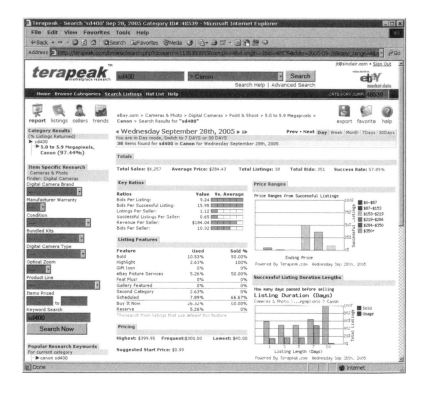

Figure 27.4 Results of a search for a Canon SD400 digital camera, Report page, on Terapeak. ©2005 AERS, Inc. All rights reserved.

Figure 27.5 Results of a search for a Canon SD400 digital camera, Listings page, on Terapeak. ©2005 AERS, Inc. All rights reserved.

The Trends page gives you a graph of the dollar-volume sales trends and successful listings. It also gives you total sales, average price, total listings, total bids, and success rates, truly a gold mine of information.

Using the Hot List

Now we're talking! What's hot? The Terapeak Hot List will tell you with ratings of Hot, Very Hot, and Super Hot. We found a Minolta SLR X-series (film camera and lenses) high on the Hot List for the past year (Hot rating). We looked at the Trends page, which showed a slight downward trend (see Figure 27.6). This is a hot item at a time when film cameras are on the way out (being replaced by digital cameras), so the slight downward trend was understandable. What's amazing is that a film camera could still be hot in 2005. Who knew? But Terapeak tells all.

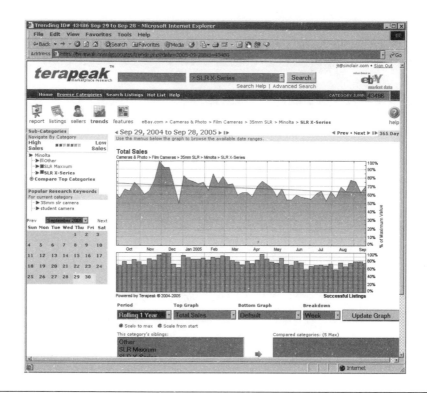

Figure 27.6 Trends page on Terapeak for sale of the Minolta SLR X-series camera (and accessories) for one year. ©2005 AERS, Inc. All rights reserved.

You can elect to rank the Hot List by Sales Rank, Status, or Success (percentage of auction success). That will lead you to some hot products.

Focus

By focusing on just marketplace analysis and not auction management services, Terapeak has made a solid name for itself as the leader in eBay research. This is a service you probably won't want to do without.

Usefulness

Now although these research programs and services are not perfect in our opinion (eBay data isn't perfect), they do provide you with some useful statistics. You need to analyze each bit of data and verify it, if possible, by a closer review. In addition, you need to eliminate certain portions of the data that you judge unreliable. What you have left is data relevant to your anticipated eBay retailing effort. Each research tool will become even more useful as you learn to master it.

Others

This is not meant to be a definitive coverage of what's available in marketplace research for eBay retailers. These are just four examples. Get on the Web and survey the list of auction management services in Chapter 4 to see what each has to offer in the way of research.

eBay Auction Management Services

eBay competes with third-party (independent) vendors to provide its own auction management software and services. Naturally, because it has the data, it also provides statistical information. Hence, you can mine eBay's data through eBay's services.

Seller Central Services

On eBay, go Sell, Seller Central to access resources for selling on eBay. Under What's Hot you can use: Hot Items by Category, which shows where demand is outpacing supply; eBay Pulse, which shows trends in eBay searches; or the Merchandising Calendar, which gives notice of upcoming eBay seasonal promotions.

Under Advanced Selling you can use eBay Sales Reports to analyze your own sales with an eye to what works and what doesn't. If you have an eBay Store, it includes eBay Sales Reports and also Traffic Reports, which you can use to analyze your visitor traffic for specific items.

Completed Listings

For every auction category there is a Completed Listings filter. eBay archives many weeks of completed auctions and enables member access. By using this filter, you can access the completed auctions—the done deals. The Completed Listings generate, in effect, the market prices for each category. It doesn't get any more certain than this.

Completed Listings are now used far beyond eBay to determine the market prices of products. For instance, offline appraisers and auction-eers rely on Completed Listings. Where else in the world can they go to get such accurate market (price) information?

This is a golden tool for you to determine the prices at which you can expect to sell products on eBay. The prices you can expect to get for the products you anticipate selling is one of the prime determinants of whether such sales (such products) can sustain your eBay retail business. A gussied-up version of this is included in Terapeak's analysis.

Auction Action

Your powers of observation can provide you with an awesome tool. Get on eBay and observe what's going on!

OK, you have a few ideas about what products you might want to sell and you want to know more. Can you sell the items profitably? Go on eBay and observe the auction action. You don't have to bid—just watch.

- Is the market for the items too crowded?
- How much merchandise is sold each week?
- What are the selling prices for the items?
- Who are the competitors?
- How competent are the competitors?
- Are there opportunities for expanding sales as outlined in Chapter 1?
- Are there other similar products that may sell better?

You can't make this a scientific study. But you can make it a systematic study. Develop a template for an observation sheet. When you observe, fill in the sheet. By using the template, you will collect full and comparable information each time you observe. Then you can make well-considered choices between products.

Keep Your Eyes Open

Observation time is a good time to keep your eyes open. In observing eBay, you may inadvertently find other products to sell that you had not thought of.

Test-Market

This is the simplest and best technique for determining whether your product choices will sell. Test-market (sell) them on eBay. There are a couple of things to remember in doing this:

- Make sure your fulfillment operation is ready to handle the sales. You don't want to get negative feedback.

- Be ready to provide great customer service.

- Use drop shipping, if practical, to avoid commencing a fulfillment operation.

- Don't go overboard. Sell small quantities of items.

- Experiment with different starting bids, reserves, and Buy-It-Now prices.

- Experiment with different categories, titles, and auction ads (advanced test-marketing).

- Keep detailed written records for later analysis.

- Use a research service or an auction management service with reporting capability to analyze sales.

There are two ways to approach test-marketing. First, carefully test-market products individually one at a time, keep careful records, and conduct an ongoing review for your test-marketing activities.

Second, just start selling items as you plan to sell them routinely. This approach will probably lead you to selling in greater quantities. At the end of a specific period (e.g., one month), use the report capabilities of your auction management service to analyze your sales in the greatest detail possible.

Keep Your Eyes Open Again

Test-marketing is a good time to keep your eyes open. In analyzing eBay, you may inadvertently find other products to sell that you had not thought of.

Google

Figure out the keywords related to the products you want to sell, and you can find out other similar words with Google's Adwords Keyword Tool (*https://adwords.google.com/select/KeywordSandbox*). This gives you more keywords to consider in chosing the ones to use for your products in Google's adword advertising system.

You can use Google adwords to test products (i.e., by creating ads for the products and receiving orders at a website or at an eBay Store). You can find out shortly whether there's a market for your products.

Also check out Google Alerts. You pick the keywords, and Google emails you any news regarding the keywords. It's great for getting new ideas and even for finding out what competitors are doing.

Yahoo

Yahoo Search Marketing (*http://searchmarketing.yahoo.com*) is another place for indirect product research. You can get statistics about the number of searches for certain keywords and the companies bidding to advertise on the keywords. It also suggests related keywords. This can be a useful indicator of supply and demand. Yahoo! also issues alerts.

Beyond Yahoo

There are hundreds of search engines, and you might want to investigate any that specialize in fields relevant to your products. If one provides relevant statistics, such statistics might be excellent information for doing some fruitful analysis.

At *http://www.pixelfast.com/overture* (see Figure 27.7) you can see the bidding for keywords and the number of searches done on keywords. It can be useful to see them together.

Market Research Services

There are many market research services that serve corporations and large retailers. They are expensive. They may be able to help you choose products to sell online if you can afford the fees. This approach is not one that most new eBay retailers will take. Nonetheless, this approach may be cost-effective for you in some situations.

Offline

Before the Web, the statistical data available on sales was robust in the print media. It continues to be robust with statistics published by manufacturers, trade organizations, consulting firms, periodicals (newspapers, magazines, newsletters, and trade publications), and even governments. The Web is a good place to start, but don't overlook your local library.

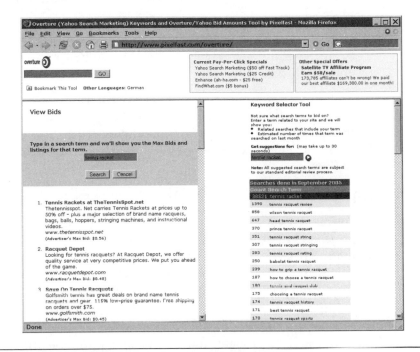

Figure 27.7 Overture (Yahoo) and Pixelfast webpage.

Also offline are the trade shows. Chapter 9 covers them. There are a lot of manufacturers and wholesalers at the trade shows. Most of them have done their market research homework. You can get a wealth of information just by talking with as many people as possible. You can learn about new trends and even spot new trends. You may even be able to pick up some free research (e.g., written reports).

Saturation

Use the auction observation technique (and others) above to test for niche saturation. You can't make money on eBay in a niche saturated with sellers and products. You just can't. Find a niche with a market where demand appears to exceed supply.

The fallacy published in many books about eBay is that if you can find a popular niche, you can jump in and make money. Unfortunately, that is seldom the case. Most popular niches are saturated with sales. That means price wars. And price wars mean unprofitable sales for most sellers.

Instead, your focus needs to be on seeking a popular category and then finding within such a category a subcategory niche where demand appears to exceed supply.

Remember too, that statistics tell only what has been sold. These statistics can't find new niches. New niches are in the future. The way to find a new niche is to find a need and discover through your research that such a need is unfilled. Then fill it by selling into a new niche that you create.

Summary

You have a variety of choices for doing your research. Use as many as possible. Measure supply and demand. You can't do it perfectly, but in many cases you can get an accurate idea of what's going on in the market. If it appears that demand is greater than supply, try some test-marketing with the products you want to sell. Or if you are trying to identify products that will sell, try some test-marketing with products that are appropriate for the market. In either case, if the products sell well, you have probably found yourself a profitable niche.

Epilogue

As you have read, this book is about inventory—how to identify, choose, and find items to sell on eBay. It isn't a book about starting or revving up an eBay business. You can find a generous amount of information on that topic in *eBay Business the Smart Way,* Second Edition, a book specifically written for beginning eBay retailers.

Nor is this book about marketing your products and business. *Building your eBay Traffic the Smart Way* covers a lot of ground for you on that topic, including datafeed marketing, a powerful new technique that you will be reading more about soon. (Datafeed marketing is sometimes mistakenly referred to as "channel marketing.")

To sell your inventory on eBay or anywhere, you need to write clear copy (product descriptions). *Building Your eBay Traffic the Smart Way* also will help you with that task. In addition, you need to supply good product photographs to your prospective buyers. *eBay Photography the Smart Way* will teach you easy, efficient, and effective product photography—that's right, not just photography but *product* photography.

Of course, one easy way to increase your eBay sales is to sell to customers abroad. But that's not covered comprehensively in this book either.

Read *eBay Global the Smart Way* for a thorough treatment of that topic.

If you haven't mastered the eBay basics yet, try *eBay the Smart Way,* Fourth Edition, written for buyers and sellers alike. And if you haven't taken advantage of the largest used car marketplace in the world yet, read *eBay Motors the Smart Way.*

With all these books, you might be getting the idea that eBay isn't a get-rich-quick scheme. That's so true. eBay presents you with a fantastic opportunity to start a profitable retail business with a minimal amount of capital. But you will likely have to work hard to earn a profit. And you will need all the help (information) you can get in order to become financially successful.

For more information and updates to these books visit BaysideBusiness at *http://baysidebusiness.com.*

What does the future hold for you? Well, the dot-com boom raised expectations to the heavens. Then the dot-com bust led many to believe that ecommerce was dead. The truth is that ecommerce is booming. It's not meeting the impossible expectations set during the dot-com boom. Nonetheless, it's increasing substantially each year. If any other sector of the economy were increasing as fast, it would be front page news. But the dot-com bust has made the substantial increases in ecommerce each year somehow old news.

Remember always, it's better to be in a booming sector of the economy than in a stagnant sector. And with eBay you are right in the middle of the action.

Good luck.

Appendix The Top 13 Tips for Finding eBay Inventory

Top 13 tips for sellers who want to find high-quality and profitable products to sell in their eBay retail businesses.

1. **Research** The only way to find good products to sell is research. It's work. If you don't do this work, you won't find the most profitable products.

2. **Product Profit Model** Use the Product Profit Model to choose products to sell. You will be happier and make more profit too.

3. **Customer Service** The three most important things in retailing are: (1) customer service, (2) customer service, and (3) customer service. When acquiring inventory, keep customer service in

mind. You don't want inventory that will prevent you from giving great customer service to your buyers.

4. **Cost-effectiveness** Take cost-effectiveness into consideration when choosing inventory. The wholesale price is not the only consideration. For instance, don't overlook the cost of customer service.

5. **Test Market** Sell a product in small quantities before commiting to selling it long term.

6. **Drop Shipping** Consider drop shipping to see if it's right for you. At the least, it may be a good way for you to get started. It's also a great way to test products and eBay categories without the cost and risk of adding to your inventory.

7. **Relationships** Understand the supplier-retailer chain of relationships. Endeavor to maintain good relations with suppliers.

8. **Negotiate** The three best ways to deal with suppliers are: (1) negotiate, (2) negotiate, and (3) negotiate.

9. **Credit** Establish and maintain good credit. Being able to order inventory on supplier credit will save you money (capital).

10. **Inventory Management Software** Dedicate yourself to learning and using the inventory management module of an auction management service.

11. **Just-In-Time Inventory** Strive to operate a just-in-time inventory system. Your capital investment will be lower.

12. **Trade Shows** Attend national trade shows. That's where the opportunities are.

13. **Go Global, Go Local** Import inventory from abroad directly. The Internet has made foreign trade easier than in the past. On the other hand, don't overlook local sources of inventory that may not be known to competitors outside your locale.

Glossary

Some of the terms we use in the book are defined below for your convenient reference.

auction management service
This is a package of retail business management software used via the Web in your browser. Some components are downloaded and used in your computer. Auction management services and auction management software are essentially the same.

auction management software
This is a package of retail business management software used in your computer. Some components are used via the Web in your browser.

bundling
Adding minor products from manufacturers to a sales package that

includes a primary product. You pay nominal prices for the products supplied by manufacturers intenting to promote such products.

consumer show

A commerce show that is put on primarily for consumers.

Craig's List

A local online marketplace now present in over 100 cities worldwide.

credit terms

The credit a supplier extends to you to pay for inventory. Credit terms are usually 5 days (Net 5), 15 days (Net 15), or 30 days (Net 30).

datafeed marketing

You use the database in an auction management service to list your inventory items. You can upload your items to a marketplace such as Froogle with a simple datafeed (data exported from a database).

distribution

A manufacturer typically distributes its products to wholesalers, also known as distributors. Wholesalers in turn distribute the products to retailers that sell the products to consumers.

drop shipper

A manufacturer or wholesaler that ships products ordered by retailers for their customers directly to the customers.

drop shipping

The act of a manufacturer or wholesaler sending a product directly to a consumer who is a customer of a retailer.

Froogle

Google's ecommerce catalog of merchandise. Once you sign up to be a seller (free), you upload your items to Froogle with a simple datafeed.

fulfillment

That part of your retail operation that packs and ships products.

inventory

The products, goods, and merchandise that you stock and sell. Also the merchandise that you have drop shipped to your buyers.

inventory turns

When you sell your entire inventory, it is said to turn over once. The goal is to turn over your inventory as many times as possible within a specified period (e.g., one year).

just-in-time inventory

With careful planning and reliable shipping by the supplier, you can keep your inventory levels as low as possible without running short. This also keeps your capital requirements for inventory low.

keystone

A keystone markup is 100 percent (i.e., a 50 percent margin).

MAP

Short for Minimum Advertised Price, this is the price set by a manufacturer for a product in advertising agreements with retailers. The agreements are enforceable thus controlling the price indirectly.

margin

The margin is that percentage of the retail price earned by a retailer, typically 40 or 50 percent.

markup

The markup is that percentage of the wholesale price that is added to set the retail price, typically 67 to 100 percent.

MSRP

Short for Manufacturer's Suggested Retail Price, this is the retail price set by a manufacturer. It is not binding on a retailer due to the prohibition against price-fixing by the antitrust laws.

packaging

Adding minor products to a sales package that includes a primary product. You pay wholesale prices for the add-on products.

picking
Shopping for items to be sold to a retailer for resale.

product cycle
The four-stage cycle (introduction, growth, maturity, and decline) that a typical product goes through.

product profit model
A simple financial model that shows how much profit a single item makes. It helps you to identify products worth your time and effort and to avoid products that aren't worth the trouble.

retail
This term denotes sales to the public at the highest prices in the distribution chain. The MSRP is the retail price set by a manufacturer. The "street price" is the retail price actually paid by most consumers, often a discount from MSRP.

sales tax license
A license issued to you by your state for collecting sales tax (on products you sell in your state) and remitting it to the state.

trade mart
A permanent facility that admits only suppliers and retailers. Your sales tax license is usually your ticket for admission.

trade show
A commerce show that admits only suppliers and retailers. Your sales tax license is usually your ticket for admission.

wholesale
This term denotes sales to retailers at wholesale prices. Wholesale prices vary depending on the volume that a retailer buys.

wholesaler
A distributor that buys from manufacturers and sells to retailers.

Index

265

The Definitive Series on eBay!

Comprehensive and Easy to Use!
Affordably Priced—A Lot of Information, All for $25 or less!

eBay the Smart Way
Selling, Buying, and Profiting on the Web's #1 Auction Site, Fourth Edition
0-8144-7289-3 $17.95

eBay Business the Smart Way
Maximize Your Profits on the Web's #1 Auction Site, Second Edition
0-8144-7267-2 $24.95

eBay Motors the Smart Way
Selling and Buying Cars, Trucks, Motorcycles, Boats, Parts, Accessories,
and Much More on the Web's #1 Auction Site
0-8144-7252-4 $17.95

eBay Global the Smart Way
Buying and Selling Internationally on the World's #1 Auction Site
0-8144-7241-9 $19.95

Building Your eBay Traffic the Smart Way
Use Froogle, Data Feeds, Cross-Selling, Advance Listing Strategies,
and More to Boost Your Sales on the Web's #1 Auction Site
0-8144-7269-9 $17.95

eBay Photography the Smart Way
Creating Great Product Pictures That Will Attract Higher Bids
and Sell Your Items Faster
0-8144-7293-1 $19.95

For more information about these titles, sneak previews of the contents, and updates
on forthcoming titles, check out **www.amacombooks.org/ebaysmartway**.

Available from your local retailer or online at Amazon.com, bn.com, and other
online bookstores.

Prices subject to change.

BOSTON PUBLIC LIBRARY

3 9999 05096 696 7

Codman Sq. Branch Library
690 Washington Street
Dorchester, MA 02124-3511

WITHDRAWN
No longer the property of the
Boston Public Library.
Sale of this material benefited the Library